Anonymous

Returns of Desertions, Discharges, Deaths, etc.,

in Maine regiments for the months of August, September and October,

1864

Anonymous

Returns of Desertions, Discharges, Deaths, etc.,
in Maine regiments for the months of August, September and October, 1864

ISBN/EAN: 9783337403324

Printed in Europe, USA, Canada, Australia, Japan

Cover: Foto ©Suzi / pixelio.de

More available books at **www.hansebooks.com**

RETURNS

OF

DESERTIONS, DISCHARGES, DEATHS, ETC.,

IN

MAINE REGIMENTS,

FOR THE MONTHS OF

AUGUST, SEPTEMBER AND OCTOBER,

1864.

RETURNS

FOR

AUGUST, SEPTEMBER AND OCTOBER.

List of desertions, discharges, deaths, &c., of enlisted men in Maine Regiments and Corps for the months of August, September and October, 1864, as reported in the monthly returns received at the Adjutant General's Office for those months.

FIRST REGIMENT CAVALRY.

August, 1864.

Discharged.

Names.	Co.	Date.	Remarks.
W S Collins	E	July 18, 1864	For promotion.
James C Ring	F	Aug. 9,	For disability.
Peter Benbnger	K	" 31,	To enter U. S. Navy.

Deceased.

Names.	Co.	Date.	Remarks.
Joseph McAlister	B	July 22, 1864	Of disease.
James Carroll	B	Aug. 30,	do
B C Payson	C	July 6,	do
Henry McCurdy	D	Aug. 25,	do
H W Beston	H	" 29,	From wounds received in action.
C M Chalborne	I	" 26,	do
J D Thompson	K	" 16,	Killed in action.
B F Barnes	I	" 18,	do
S H Murphy	I	" 18,	do
Wm S McClunning	G	" 16,	do
Sam'l Levanseler	G	" 25,	do
George E Reed	G	" 25,	do
Axsel Smith	E	" 16,	do
Wm B Baker	D	" 11,	From wounds received in action.
Jerome Bidley	C	" 21,	do

September, 1864.

Deserted.

Names.	Co.	Date.	Remarks.
Henry A Jackson	H	Sept. 19, 1864	
John Robinson	K		From Distribution Camp

Discharged.

Names.	Co.	Date.	Remarks.
Lorenzo White	F	Sept. 3, 1864	For promotion.
Levi Lurllen	L	" 17,	do

FIRST REGIMENT CAVALRY, (Continued.)

Deceased.

Names.	Co.	Date.	Remarks.
Daniel R Laugpher	B	Sept. 3, 1864.	From wounds received in action.
John Ford	C	Aug. 13,	Of disease.
George W Patten	D	Sept. 24,	do
George W Brown	E	Aug. 24,	do
W P Smith	F	July 21,	do
J W Bray	G	Aug. 14,	Killed in action.
L B Spaulding	G	Sept. 28,	Of disease.
Walter Drew	H	Mar. 18,	Killed in action.
L L Heal	H	Aug. 23,	do
Wm A Young	H	June 2,	From wounds received in action.
Cyrus M Russell	H	Mar. 15,	Of disease.
Wm E Foster	H	Sept. 29,	Killed in action.
Wm H Drew	K	Aug. 16,	Of disease.
Seth H Weymouth	M	Sept. 19,	From wounds received in action.

Transferred.

Henry Johnson	F	Dec. —, 1863.	To V. R. Corps.
A L Douglass	L	May 1, 1864.	To signal corps.

OCTOBER, 1864.

Deserted.

Henry J Tate	B	April 30, 1864.	While on furlough.

Discharged.

George H Higgins	C	Sept. 29, 1864.	For disability.
Joel Wilson	F	Oct. 10,	For promotion.
L Copeland	H		For disability.
Thomas Ring	K	Oct. 16,	do

Deceased.

G S McCorrison	B		Of disease.
A F Prince	B		do
E C Porter	B		do
Isaac B Conant	C	Aug. 25, 1864.	do
Oscar O Richardson	E	Oct. 27,	Killed in action.
A E Knight	E	" 27,	do
E E Decker	E	" 20,	Of disease.
F M Shaw	F		do
G K Estes	G	Oct. 27,	Killed in action.
M Libbey	G	" 27,	do
J B Johnson	I	" 2,	Of disease.
Frank Harris	K	" 27,	Killed in action.
Robert Lang	K	" 27,	do
Charles Lang	K	" 27,	do
Wm Staples	K	" 27,	do
Ivory Ross	K	Sept. 11,	Of disease.
John B Thomas	L		do
Rufus H Wingate	M	Aug. 28,	From wounds received in action.

N. B.—Companies D, F, G, H, I, K, L, M, of the First Regiment D. C. Cavalry (Baker's) were transferred to the First Regiment Maine Cavalry, and the members thereof will hereafter appear in the latter regiment.

SECOND REGIMENT CAVALRY.

August, 1864.

Deserted.

Names.	Co.	Date.	Remarks.
Peter Roberts	H	Aug. 23, 1864.	At Barrancas, Fla.
Levi Dickinson	F	" 3,	At Algiers, La.

Discharged.

Names.	Co.	Date.	Remarks.
Eugene Shaw	A	Aug. 10, 1864.	For disability.
Arthur N Davis	C	" 11,	
John Stevens	C	" 16,	
Benj R Jones	D	" 27,	For promotion.
Simeon B Cushman	F	" 17,	For disability.
Moses C West	H	" 17,	do
George L Cole	I	" 11,	do
Ellis W Ayer	I	" 27,	For promotion.

Deceased.

Names.	Co.	Date.	Remarks.
Ebenezer Bigger	A	Aug. 1, 1864.	At New Orleans, La.
J S Arey	B	" 24,	At Barrancas, Fla.
Edwin Miner	B	" 29,	do
Amos Keller	C	" 18,	do
Joseph Pinkham	C	" 21,	do
A D Libbey	C	" 31,	do
Geo M Mullen	D	" 27,	At Augusta, Me.
Lewis M Crummett	D	June 24,	At Baton Rouge, La.
Thos L Whitten	D	July —,	At New Orleans, La.
Thos S B Judkins	D	Aug. 9,	do
Orrin B Ward	D	" 10,	do
Ellis Morrison	D	" 10,	do
Lorenzo J Hall	D	" 10,	do
Wm H Ball	D	" 26,	At Barrancas, Fla.
Geo H Bagley	D	" 29,	do
Warren Reed	F	" 1,	At Greenville, La.
John Q Pease	F	" 7,	At Warrenton, Fla.
Gilbert Stetson	F	" 7,	At New Orleans, La.
Benj F Tibbetts	F	" 11,	At Barrancas, Fla.
Orlando Young	F	" 15,	do
Benjamin W Norton	F	" 27,	do
Charles E Hawes	F	" 27,	At New Orleans, La.
Greenleaf Smart	G	" 21,	At Barrancas, Fla.
Joseph B Day	H	" 18,	do
Nathan H Cousens	H	" 19,	do
Wm Gilchrist	H	July 22,	At Augusta, Me.
James M Gee	I	Aug. 11,	At Barrancas, Fla.
Amaziah Young	I	" 11,	do
Eugene Millett	I	" 21,	do
Wm B Field	K	July 24,	At New Orleans, La.
Adoniram J Taylor	K	Aug. 9,	At Barrancas, Fla.
Reuel W Fish	K	" 31,	do
Edwin K Jordan	K		At New Orleans, La.
Albert Pushor	K		do
O F Ham	L	Aug. 21,	At Barrancas, Fla.
John Spurr	M	" 1,	At New Orleans, La.
Charles E Rand	M	" 2,	do
Daniel B Bean	M	" —,	do
Franklin B Huntoon	M	" 22,	At Barrancas, Fla.
John A Jones	M	" 21,	do

SECOND REGIMENT CAVALRY, (Continued.)

Transferred.

Names.	Co.	Date.	Remarks.
Robert H Sinclair	A	Aug. 1, 1864.	To U. S. Navy.
Samuel K Doe	B	do	do
Geo W Chamberlain	B	do	do
B. F Brookings	B	do	do
Charles White	B	do	do
John Babcock	B	do	do
Horace Bowring	B	do	do
S H Eldridge	B	do	do
Charles Jellison	B	do	do
E E Lowell	B	do	do
N C Moore	B	do	do
W H McIntyre	B	do	do
W H Oliver	B	do	do
A Parker	B	do	do
Charles Sabine	B	do	do
H N Dexter	B	do	do
John Edgecomb	C	do	do
Daniel Black	C	do	do
Rufus C Gerry	C	do	do
Joseph H Goodwin	C	do	do
Luther Oliver	C	do	do
Moses A Ware	C	do	do
Amasa R Meador	C	do	do
Thomas E Sinclair	D	Aug. 12, 1864.	To V. R. Corps.
David R Ginn	E	Aug. 1,	To U. S. navy.
Samuel Hoffman	E	do	do
Edgar A Hanakay	E	do	do
Wm J Brown	E	do	do
Geo A Dill	E	do	do
David M Robbins	E	do	do
Wm Wasgatt	E	do	do
Harrison Emery	E	do	do
Samuel W Hewett	E	do	do
Charles H Leighton	E	do	do
Chas O Wentworth	E	do	do
George Hall	E	do	do
Melzer T Dyer	E	do	do
David F Hysom	E	do	do
Charles T Gould	E	Aug. 12, 1864.	To V. R. Corps.
John E Dow	F	Aug. 1,	To U. S. Navy.
Charles J Roberts	F	do	do
Burton Bunker	G	do	do
Chas S Trowbridge	G	do	do
John Fogg	G	do	do
George Brackett	G	do	do
Edward Billings	H	do	do
Alden Carr	H	do	do
Ephraim L Emerson	H	do	do
Byron A Hart	H	do	do
George T Randlett	H	do	do
Stephen S Smith	H	do	do
Walter L Boynton	I	do	do
Benj A Merrill	I	do	do
Otis Gray	K	do	do
Thomas Gray	K	do	do
Alonzo D Moore	K	do	do

SECOND REGIMENT CAVALRY, (Continued.)

Transferred.

Names.	Co.	Date.	Remarks.
Wilson Blake	K	Aug. 1, 1864.	To U. S. Navy.
Edward Leighton	K	do	do
James H Brown	L	do	do
Thomas W Crowell	L	do	do
Daniel Donnelly	L	do	do
John G Hanscom	L	do	do
Adam McCulloch	L	do	do
Cyrus Southard	L	do	do
Chandler Peavy	L	do	do
Wm H Wentworth	L	do	do
John Doherty	L	do	do
Wm Longpre	L	do	do
Thos A Richardson	L	do	do
George S Pillsbury	L	do	do

SEPTEMBER, 1864.

Erratum.

Elwin Dillingham	G		Was erroneously reported deceased June 5, '64, in Return for June '64.

Deceased.

William Morgridge	A	Aug. 14, 1864.	At St. Louis, Mo.
Abraham Gerow	A	" 23,	At Barrancas, Fla.
Henry A Mann	A	" 26,	do
Samuel Bradbury	A	Sept. 23,	At Fort Gaines, Ala.
Alexander Bigger	A	Aug. 28,	At New York.
M P Philbrick	B	Sept. 12,	At Barrancas, Fla.
W S Elwell	B	" 29,	do
Calvin N Brann	C	" 5,	do
Geo M Garland	C	" 6,	do
Willis J James	C	" 12,	do
Frederick E Gowell	C	" 15,	do
Gardiner M Fuller	C	" 27,	do
Robert J Kitchen	C	" 30,	do
John C Thompson	D	" 1,	do
John E Richards	D	" 3,	do
Rishworth A Ward	D	" 7,	do
Cassius C Dodge	D	" 11,	At New Orleans, La.
Barzilla B Greeley	D	" 12,	At Barrancas, Fla.
Daniel W Barker	D	" 21,	do
Wm C Hall	E	" 15,	do
Asa Robbins	E	" 22,	do
Joseph W Newbert	E	" 27,	do
Silas Campbell	F	" 27,	Killed in action.
E Erwin Wright	F	" 4,	At Barrancas, Fla.
Theodore S Sprague	F	" 8,	do
Marcus M Godfrey	F	" 12,	do
Sullivan Abbott	F	" 13,	do
Charles G Smith	F	" 15,	do
Marcellus H Merrick	F	" 17,	do
Frederick F Hussey	F	" 19,	do
Sidney E Kingsbury	F	" 21,	do
John A Abbott	F	" 24,	do
John W Vanworth	G	" 5,	At New Orleans, La.
Warren Spearin	G	" 15,	do

SECOND REGIMENT CAVALRY, (Continued.)

Deceased.

Names.	Co.	Date.	Remarks.
George Pooler	G	Sept. 14, 1864.	At Barrancas, Fla.
Joseph F Fields	G	" 24,	do
Charles E Porter	H	" 18,	do
James Knichler	H	" 18,	do
Daniel J West	H	" 18,	do
David B Carter	H	" 26,	do
John Smith	I	Aug. 8,	At New Orleans, La.
Charles O Crosby	I	" 12,	do
Fred H Seavey	I	" 31,	At Barrancas, Fla.
James H Whitmore	I	Sept. 3,	do
Roscoe G Lindsey	I	" 8,	do
Lemuel Reynolds	I	" 8,	do
Charles F Houston	I	" 11,	do
Charles Haskell	I	" 18,	do
Charles F Knight	I	" 26,	do
Charles K Stowell	I	Aug. 18,	At New Orleans, La.
Eugene A Smith	I	Sept. 22,	do
Daniel Maguire	K	" 19,	At Barrancas, Fla.
Clarkson Jones	K	" 22,	do
William H Smart	K	" 22,	do
Edward Hackett	K	" 28,	do
Samuel S Snell	K	" 29,	do
Thomas A Davis	L	" 27,	Killed in action.
John Robinson	L	" 25,	At Barrancas, Fla.
James K Bolton	L	" 28,	do
Albert Moore jr	M	" 1,	do
Eli Garland	M	" 5,	do
Jacob J Byron	M	" 14,	do
Bradford Pickens	M	" 17,	do
Daniel Ray	M	" 18,	do
William Taylor	M	" 19,	do
Charles H Batchelder	M	" 20.	do
George H Butler	M	" 22,	do
Enos Dow	M	" 24,	do
Fred W Starbird	M	" 28,	do

Missing.

Henry O Neal	D	Sept. 28, 1864.	On the march.
Abial N Linscott	E	" 27,	In action.
Henry Brown	E	" 27,	do
Daniel Ellis	H	" 27,	do
Chester Whiting	I	" 27,	do
G W Williams	I	" 27,	do

OCTOBER, 1864.

Discharged.

Ira F Wadlin	A	Aug. 20, 1864.	For disability.
Joseph Brewster	D	Sept. 17,	
Oakman F Glidden	E	" 1,	For promotion.
Nelson Millett	I	" 15,	For disability.

Deceased.

Jeremiah Farwell	A	Sept. 12, 1864.	At Barrancas, Fla.
Chas W Kimball	A	" 14,	do
John A Mullen	A	" 15,	do

SECOND REGIMENT CAVALRY, (Continued.)

Deceased.

Names.	Co	Date.	Remarks.
Josiah M Morse	A	Sept. 10, 1864.	At New Orleans, La.
Ira Morrill	A	July 28,	do
George H Bagley	A	Aug. 28,	At Barrancas, Fla.
Geo B Atwood	B	Oct. 6,	do
Thos H Nockton	B	" 20,	At New Orleans, La.
Charles W Allen	B	" 13,	do
Asa Holman	C	Aug. 2,	do
Daniel Hutchinson	C	" 4,	do
John B Keen	C	" 2,	do
Hiram A Mills	C	" 4,	do
Edward E Worth	C	" 23,	do
Charles O Watson	C	Oct. 1,	At Barrancas, Fla.
Elisha Atkinson	D	Sept. 19,	At New Orleans, La.
John Q A Bowen	D	Oct. 21,	At Barrancas, Fla.
Eugene Cate	D	" 9,	At New Orleans, La.
Eugene Foss	D	Sept. 18,	At Alexandria, La.
M Erskine	E	Oct. 9,	At Barrancas, Fla.
Ambrose Dill	E	" 10,	At New Orleans, La.
Joseph G Ellis	F	Sept. 11,	do
John Burbank	F	" 24,	do
Oscar A Rogers	G	Aug. 21,	do
Edward P Hanscom	H	" 11,	do
Oscar Richards	H	" 22,	do
James O Snow	H	" 29,	do
Solomon J Gray	H	" —,	do
Marcellus B Porter	H	Oct. 5,	do
Rufus B Ladd	H	" 8,	do
William O Bean	H	" 8,	do
Jacob Emery	I	Aug. 24,	On ship board.
Hubbard R Wing	I	Sept. 1,	At Winthrop, Me.
Apollo Hammond	I	" 29,	At New Orleans, La.
Samuel D Besse	I	Oct. 1,	At Barrancas, Fla.
Hosea Harlow	I	" 5,	do
Samuel Stewart	I	" 15,	At New Orleans, La.
Joseph H Casey	K	" 8,	At Barrancas, Fla.
Andrew G Hanson	K	" 9,	At New Orleans, La.
Edwin V Page	K	" 17,	do
John Brawn	K	" 23,	At Barrancas, Fla.
Thos W Lee	K	" 28,	do
John H Kingsbury	L	" 24,	do
Geo F Rankins	M	" 1,	do
Orrin L Seco	M	" 11,	do
James Emery	M	Aug. 16,	At New Orleans, La.
Chas C Works	M	Sept. 16,	At Alexandria, La.
Benj M Bradbury	M	Oct. 26,	At Barrancas, Fla.
Charles W Palmer	M	Aug. 20,	At New Orleans, La.

Missing.

Moses Sims	M	Sept. 27, 1864.	In action.

2

FIRST REGIMENT HEAVY ARTILLERY.

MAY, 1864.

Deserted.

Names.	Co.	Date.	Remarks.
Robert Wooster	A	May 15, 1864.	At Fort Simmons.
Wm S Mayville	B	" 28,	At Fort Mansfield.
Warren H Newell	B	" 15,	do
John T Sears	D	" 14,	At Fort Sumner, Md.
Wm H Harmon	E	" 17,	do
Sewall Larrabee	F	" 2,	In Maine.
Arthur D Chase	L	" 15,	Not ret'd at expiration of furlough.

Deceased.

Names.	Co.	Date.	Remarks.
Daniel W Snow	A	May 19, 1864.	Killed in action.
Addison C Percival	B	" 19,	do
R P Crowell	B	" 19,	do
Austin Q French	B	" 19,	do
Warren M Brown	B	" 19,	do
George B Robinson	B	" 19,	do
Herbert T Gibbs	B	" 19,	do
Jethro W Clark	B	" 19,	do
Nathan A Hopkins	B	" 19,	do
James McGrath	B	" 19,	do
John C Erskine	B	" 19,	do
L B Whitney	B	" 19,	do
E H Wasgatt	C	" 19,	do
John P Higgins	C	" 19,	do
George Merrill	C	" 19,	do
Christopher C Myrick	C	" 19,	do
George W Burns	C	" 19,	do
Harrison Fogg	C	" 19,	do
Geo W Smith	C	" 19,	do
Everett E Emery	C	" 19,	do
Edwin C Marcyes	C	" 19,	do
Isaac C Staples	C	" 19,	do
Eben W Foster	C	" 19,	do
Wm H Campbell	C	" 19,	do
Sidney S Eldridge	C	" 19,	do
Charles Shaw	D	" 11,	Of disease.
Chas W Smith	D	" 21,	From wounds received in action.
Geo A Veskend	D	" 22,	Killed while on picket.
Chas H Parshley	E	" 19,	Killed in action.
Cyrus S Labree	E	" 19,	do
Emerson Bartlett	E	" 19,	do
Joseph F Brown	E	" 19,	do
Seth H Brown	E	" 19,	do
Charles W Hanson	E	" 19,	do
Flavil B Jackson	E	" 19,	do
Francis D Lindsey	E	" 19,	do
Leander Nixon	E	" 19,	do
Davis G Brown	F	" 19,	do
F C Baswell	F	" 19,	do
C R Clark	F	" 19,	do
A H Chick	F	" 19,	do
T L May	F	" 19,	do
H L Mitchell	F	" 19,	do
Frank Voyer	F	" 19,	do
A Patterson	F	" 19,	do
Alphonso Smith	F	" 20,	From wounds received in action.

FIRST REGIMENT HEAVY ARTILLERY, (Continued.)

Deceased.

Names.	Co.	Date.	Remarks.
A S Young	F	May 20, 1864.	From wounds received in action.
George A Bonzey	G	" 19,	Killed in action.
Clinton D Saunders	G	" 19,	do
William C Green	G	" 19,	do
Charles Prue	G	" 19,	do
Joseph L Downs	H	" 19,	do
Alexander Parker	H	" 19,	do
Edmund Perry	H	" 19,	do
Fernando C Plummer	H	" 31,	do
Edwin M Pratt	H	" —,	Of disease.
James H Rogers	H	" 11,	do
J D Morton	I	" 19,	Killed in action.
Benj B Soule	I	" 19,	do
Richard Dowdell	I	" 19,	do
Whitefield Mills	I	" 19,	do
Frank St Pierre	I	" 19,	do
True W Wedgwood	I	" 19,	do
Ira Chapman	I	" 19,	Of disease.
Jeremiah Loring	K	" 19,	Killed in action.
Henry W Metz	K	" 19,	do
George E Bradbury	K	" 19,	do
Samuel Collier	K	" 19,	do
James T Mack	K	" 19,	do
Franklin York	K	" 19,	do
Barzilla F Whiting	K	" 19,	do
Nathaniel Treadwell	K	" 19,	do
Field Baston	L	" 19,	do
Webster Brown	L	" 19,	do
Edwin B Chaplin	L	" 19,	do
Henry W Newman	L	" 19,	do
J Walker	L	" 19,	do
Charles E Smiley	M	" 19,	do
James Merrill	M	" 19,	do
Isaac P Davis	M	" 19,	do
Charles McMann	M	" 19,	do
Horace C Griffin	M	" 19,	do
Ira B Robbins	M	" 19,	do
Ebenezer Ordway	M	" 19,	do
Timothy Spencer	M	" 19,	do
Henry A Mitchell	M	" 19,	do

Transferred.

James Turner	A		To U. S. Navy.
Elbridge G Jordan	B	May 9, 1864.	do
Harry Bell	B	" 9,	do
Benj F Hatch	B	" 9,	do
Wm J Rand	B	" 2,	do
Casper App	B	" 15,	To const guard.
Timothy Mahoney	D	" 11,	To U. S. Navy.
Lorenzo D Fields	D	" 11,	do
George V Brown	D	" 11,	do
Warren Boynton	D	" 11,	do
Michael McDonough	D	" 15,	Ord. Sgt. at Battery Kimball.
Wm Duffey	D	" 15,	do do Vermont.
Conrad Kiosner	D	" 15,	do do Parrott.
Roscoe G Sopans	G	" 13,	To U. S. Navy.
Dennis McCabe	G	" 13,	do

FIRST REGIMENT HEAVY ARTILLERY, (Continued.)

Transferred.

Names.	Co.	Date.	Remarks.
Jeremiah Saunders	G	May 13, 1864.	To U. S. Navy.
Thos A Hodgdon	G	" 13,	do
Jefferson D Merritt	H	" 10,	do
Arthur B Tibbetts	H	" 10,	do
Geo H Norcross	H	" 10,	do
Stephen Wilcox Jr	I	" 13,	do
John Brown	I	" 13,	do
Hezekiah Gutshall	K		Ord. Sgt. to Fort Pulaski.

Missing.

Albert Dunbar	D	May 22, 1864.	
Wm Fish	E	" 19,	In action.
Albert Hayes	E	" 19,	do
Henry W Stearns	E	" 19,	do
David J Whitney	E	" 19,	do
Kenney Depray	G	" 19,	do
Charles D Terrill	G	" 31,	Taken prisoner.
Roscoe Trevett	G	" 31,	do

JUNE, 1864.

Returned from Desertion.

Turner E Davis	A		At Cold Harbor, Va.
Scribner H Davis	A		do

Deserted.

James Kingston	A		At Fort Sumner, Md.
Elias K Porter	B	June 15, 1864.	
A Thompson	C	" 10,	At Cold Harbor, Va.
A K Ayer	K	" 19,	do
J F Stinson	L		While on the march.
A D Chase	L		While on furlough.

Deceased.

Jonathan Clay Jr	A	June 18, 1864.	Killed in action.
Amasa S Flagg	A	" 18,	do
Daniel Fitzpatrick	A	" 18,	do
Thos H Griffin	A	" 22,	From wounds received in action.
John O Hughs	A	" —,	From wds. rec. in action May 19.
Cyrus A Lord	A	" 18,	Killed in action.
John Murphy	A	" 18,	do
John B Scott	A	" 18,	do
Scribner H Davis	A	" 18,	do
William Allen	B	" 20,	From wounds received in action.
Lysander Bragg	B	" 20,	do
Albert J Cole	B	" 20,	do
John Coffin	B	" 18,	Killed in action.
John Frazier	B	" 18,	do
Edward W Gorham	B	" 18,	do
James A Grant	B	" 18,	do
Henry C Hutchinson	B	" 8,	From wounds received in action.
Jacob Mudgett	B	" 20,	do
Thornton M Sears	B	May 31,	do
Franklin S Plaize	B	June 18,	Killed in action.
Wm White	B	" 18,	do
Eliot J Saulsbury	C	" 30,	From wounds received in action.

(13)

FIRST REGIMENT HEAVY ARTILLERY, (Continued.)

Deceased.

Names.	Co.	Date.	Remarks.
Milton S Beckwith	C	June 18, 1861.	Killed in action.
George Kittredge	C	" 18,	do
James M Parker	C	" 18,	do
James Cain	C	May 19,	From wounds received in action.
Charles T Clare	C	June 18,	Killed in action.
Benson Cunningham	C	" 18,	Of disease.
F G Knowlton	C	" 7,	From wounds received in action.
A Morgan	C	" 18,	Killed in action.
F Morrill	C	" 18,	do
D O Sullivan	C	" 18,	do
J Williams	C	" 18,	do
J P Emerson	C	" 20,	From wounds received in action.
J W Nason	C	" 18,	Killed in action.
Frank S Robinson	D	" 18,	do
J E Hurd	D	" 18,	do
Mathew Waters	D	" 18,	do
George Brown	D	" 18,	do
G W Bean	D	" 17,	do
Otis Dunbar	D	" 18,	do
E M Delano	E	May 26,	From wounds received in action.
E W Bean	E	June 1,	do
H O Smiley	E		do
John Bradford	E		do
Wilson G Cole	E		do
Cyrus B Hayes	E		do
Samuel Flanders	E	June 16,	do
A C Morton	E		do
A A Sidelinger	E	June 10,	do
Wm H Pouch	E		From wds. rec. in action June 16.
Henry N Cole	E	June 18,	Killed in action.
Robert Higgins	E	" 18,	do
Abial Fowler	E	" 5,	Of disease.
Wm Fish	E	" 8,	do
Royal H Strout	E	" 7,	do
Charles H Jones	F	May 28,	From wounds received in action.
Sylvester Drew	F	" 31,	do
Rodney J Taylor	F	June 5,	do
D B Wiggin	F	" 8,	do
Samuel Snow	F	" 9,	do
J B Holmes	F	" 7,	do
John A Morey	F	May 30,	Of disease
Henry C Wheeler	F		While on furlough.
James C Gray	F	June 18,	Killed in action.
Nathan Hanson	F	" 18,	do
Josiah Staples	F	" 18,	do
E Burrill	F	" 18,	do
Wm M Stevenson	F	" 23,	Of disease.
Geo L Stevens	G	" 16,	Killed in action.
Joel K Grant	G	" 18,	do
Albert Leach	G	" 18,	do
Lyman Carley	G	" 18,	do
W C Greene	G	" 18,	do
Asa Deane	G	" 18,	do
Nathan E Gross	G	" 18,	do
Frank Ellis	G	" 18,	do
Wm H Hagan	G	" 18,	do

FIRST REGIMENT HEAVY ARTILLERY, (Continued.)

Deceased.

Names.	Co.	Date.	Remarks.
David Uhr	G	June 18, 1864.	Killed in action.
Timothy C Atkins	G		From wounds received in action.
Howard Stratton	H	June 18, 1864.	Killed in action.
Wm Cates	H	" 18,	do
Hillman Foss	H	" 18,	do
Warren Hall	H	" ·18,	do
Leonard Lee	H	" 18,	do
Henry Grant	H	" 18,	do
Samuel Buzzle	H	" 18,	do
Calvin Holway	H	" 20,	From wounds received in action.
Andrew Blither	H	" 20,	do
Alvin S Casey	H	" 19,	do
Philander Low	H	" 12,	do
Daniel Hayes	H	" 19,	Of disease.
Samuel Ackley	H	" 15,	do
L Murray	H	" 12,	From wounds received in action.
George W Dole	I	" 20,	Killed in action.
Oval Derusha	I	" 20,	do
D S Dudley	I	" 19,	do
H H Done	I		do
Wm Grover	I		do
John A Trickey	I	June 19, 1864.	do
Albert W Tucker	I	" 19,	do
Elisha Whittaker	I	" 19,	do
R Gross	I	" 19,	do
Richard Sears	K	" 7,	do
J J Doherty	K	" 10,	From wounds received in action.
E Crowell	K	" 21,	do
Charles C Morse	L	" 19,	do
E Bowley	L	" 18,	do
John Crooker	L	" 24,	do
Austin P Griffin	L		In hospital.
Edward Hamor	L		From wounds received in action.
Stephen Harris	L		do
Wm King	L		do
W H McIntyre	L		do
L T Nickerson	L		do
Albert J Osgood	L		do
Alfred P Patterson	L		do
Henry A Patterson	L		do
Chas D Prescott	L		do
Wm F Rideout	L		do
Chas W Sanderson	L		do
Isaac Stevens	L		do
N S Stanley	L	June 18, 1864.	do
G C Cross	L	" 18,	do
L D Ramsdell	M	" 18,	Killed in action.
E Jennison	M	" 18,	do
Silas S Bennett	M	" 18,	do
T J Bickman	M	" 18,	do
A J Douglass	M	" 18,	do
M H De Wolf	M	" 18,	do
Edwin Stanton	M	" 18,	do
Levi Glidden	M	" 18,	do

FIRST REGIMENT HEAVY ARTILLERY, (Continued.)

Missing.

Names.	Co.	Date.	Remarks.
Isaac E Bowley	A	June 10, 1864.	In action.
Frederick Philbrook	A	" 10,	do
Eri Rowe	A	" 10,	do
Daniel McCurdy	A	" 18,	do
Noah Cross	A	" 22,	do
Arthur H Howard	A	" 22,	do
Geo W Tucker	A	" 22,	do
George F Marquis	B	" 18,	do
Robert Leadbetter	B	" 18,	do
Charles Colomy	B	" 18,	do
William Alexander	B	" 18,	do
Ezra R Read	B	" 18,	do
John A Whittier	B	" 18,	do
John G Remick	C	" 22,	Taken prisoner.
Alonzo Bennett	C	" 22,	do
Sewall A Bunker	C	" 22,	do
Albert C Ellis	D	" 18,	In action.
Charles Austin	D	" 18,	do
Chas F Broad	D	" 18,	do
Wm T Duther	D	" 18,	do
John S Libby	D	" 18,	do
Charles A Feavy	D	" 22,	do
Reuben W Seavey	D	" 18,	do
Horatio Downer	D	" 17,	do
F W Whittier	D	" 18,	do
Willard G Delano	E	" 18,	do
Geo G Thompson	E	" 18,	do
Amos J Withee	E	" 18,	do
J S Church	E	" 22,	do
Wm S Randlett	E	" 22,	do
Thomas Walton	K	" 18,	do
Robert Smith	K	" 18,	do
J A Burlingame	L	" 22,	do
Marcus M Allen	L	" 22,	do
F Campbell	L	" 22,	do

JULY, 1864.

Deserted.

B McDavitt	K	July 16, 1864.	While on furlough.

Deceased.

John C Ritchie	A	June 24, 1864.	From wounds received in action.
Adelbert Witham	A	July 2,	do
Samuel M Bolton	B	June 25,	do
Charles H Daggett	B	July 1,	do
William Bartlett	B	" 6,	do
John S Smith	B	" 3,	do
Alphonzo Miller	B	June 25,	do
Thomas Savage	B	" 25,	do
Amaziah Langley	B	May 27,	do
Leander F Elliott	B	June 2,	do
Charles W Allen	C	July 11,	do
Wellington Beal	C	" 17,	Of disease.
Lemuel A Smith	C	" 9,	From wounds received in action.
John Jackson	D	June 26,	do
Horace W Burleigh	D	July 16,	do

FIRST REGIMENT HEAVY ARTILLERY, (Continued.)

Deceased.

Names.	Co.	Date.	Remarks.
Harvey H Read	D	July 27, 1864.	From wounds received in action.
Wm C Chamberlain	D	" 11,	do
Thomas Hatch	D	" 13,	do
Jeremiah Cook	D	" 17,	do
Edwin R Dore	D	" 16,	do
Llewellyn K Knowlton	D	" 6,	do
Charles R Parkhurst	D	" 18,	do
Albert J Dunbar	D	May 22,	Killed on picket.
Samuel T Hiscock	E	July 5,	From wounds received in action.
Lewis P Lord	E	June 25,	do
Lewis A Sturtevant	E	" 23,	do
Ransom C Dodge	F	" 29,	do
Levi K Mayo	F	July 1,	do
John F Drew	F	" 7,	do
Samuel C Nason	F	" 4,	do
Geo A Osborn	F	" 9,	Of disease.
Mark T Amerson	F	" 5,	From wounds received in action.
Charles Larrabee	F	" 8,	do
Henry F Stubbs	F	" 19,	Of disease.
James S Keene	G	June 22,	do
Aaron Saunders	G	" 26,	From wounds received in action.
Francis A Leach	G	" 26,	do
W W Johnson	G	July 8,	Of disease.
George W Carr	G	" 10,	From wounds received in action.
Joseph Ridley	H	" 6,	Of disease.
Jeremiah Gray	H	" 5,	From wounds received in action.
John T Pinkham	H	" 11,	Of disease.
George W Burke	H	" 1,	From wounds received in action.
James A Nash	H	" 8,	do
Adelbert F Sproul	I	June 25,	do
Aaron C Merrill	I	" 22,	do
Joseph H Meader	I	July 25,	do
Charles S Bunker	I	" 20,	do
Frank L Dearborn	I	" 5,	do
Isaac J Maybury	I	" 20,	do
Job Kelley	I	" 25,	do
Jerome Mitchell	I	" 27,	do
Alexander Vancour	I	" 27,	do
Daniel Kennedy	K	" 25,	In Division Hospital.
Joseph E Rackliffe	L	" 12,	Of disease.
Oscar Storer	L	" 18,	From wounds received in action.
Omar Shaw	L	" 19,	do
Otis B Boynton	L	" 10,	do
John J Bragdon	L	" 25,	Of disease.
Geo A Tibbetts	L	" 1,	From wounds received in action.
Willard Mariam	L	" 24,	do
Daniel G Foster	L	" 7,	do
Kingsbury W Bowley	L	" 16,	do
Edwin R Clewly	M	" 11,	Of disease.
A J Knowles	M	" 16,	From wounds received in action.
Orrin M Brown	M	" 11,	do

Missing.

George A Haskins	D	May 21, 1864.	At Milford Station.

No returns received for August, September and October, 1864.

(17)

FIRST REGIMENT MOUNTED ARTILLERY.

FIRST BATTERY.

AUGUST, 1864.

Returned from Desertion.

Names.	Co.	Date.	Remarks.
Charles Decker		Aug. 23, 1864.	At Halltown, Va.
Joseph A Shea		" 29,	Charlestown, Va.

Deserted.

Wm H Balkam		Aug. 11, 1864.	At Halltown.

SEPTEMBER, 1864.

Deserted.

Ambrose Boyle		Sept. 28, 1864.	At Williamsburg, Va.
Patrick Maloney		" 28,	do
Charles Johnson		" 1,	At Portland, Me.

Deceased.

M Adams		Sept. 19, 1864.	Killed in action.
Henry W Moore		" 19,	do

OCTOBER, 1864.

Deserted.

James B Cole		Oct. 29, 1864.	Straggled on the march.

Deceased.

Israel Robinson		Oct. 19, 1864.	Killed in action.
John Johnson		" 19,	do

Transferred.

Charles H Cobb			To Vet. Res. Corps.

SECOND BATTERY.

AUGUST, 1864.

Deceased.

Claudius B Abbee		July 28, 1864.	In hospital.
Barzilla S Cobb		" 30,	do

SEPTEMBER, 1864.

No alterations.

OCTOBER, 1864.

Deserted.

Alpheus S Davis		Oct. 17, 1864.	Not rept. at expiration of furlough.

Deceased.

Dexter C Andrews		Oct. 6, 1864.	At Post Hospital.
Joseph Jackson		" 4,	do
Martin V Richardson		" 6,	do
Thomas F Wentworth		May —,	In hospital.
George W Wood		Aug. —,	do

3

FIRST REGIMENT MOUNTED ARTILLERY, (Continued.)
Transferred.

Names.	Co.	Date.	Remarks.
Lewis L Collins		Mar. —, 1864.	To United States Navy.
Thomas Devens		" —,	do

THIRD BATTERY.
Transferred from Company M, First Heavy Artillery.

AUGUST, 1864.

Deceased.

James Marson Jr   Aug. 18, 1864. Of disease.

SEPTEMBER, 1864.

Discharged.

John C Rich   Sept. 20, 1864. For disability.

Deceased.

Jas W W Carleton		Sept. 26, 1864.	Of disease at Alexandria, Va.
Benj F Glidden		" 28,	Of disease at David's Island, N. Y.

OCTOBER, 1864.

Deceased.

Sylvanus L Moore   July 12, 1864. Of disease.

FOURTH BATTERY.
JULY, 1864.

Deserted.

Mayhew N Marvel   July 16, 1864. At Baltimore, Md.

Deceased.

Jesse F Stetson   June 30, 1864. Of disease.

AUGUST, 1864.

Deceased.

Charles W Kimball   Aug. 11, 1864. Of disease.

SEPTEMBER, 1864.

Discharged.

John M Freeman   Sept. 19, 1864. For promotion.

Deceased.

Charles L Nichols		Aug. 7, 1864.	Of disease.
J. Owen Jr		" 10,	do

OCTOBER, 1864.

No alterations.

FIRST REGIMENT MOUNTED ARTILLERY, (Continued.)

FIFTH BATTERY.

August, 1864.

Deserted.

Names.	Co.	Date.	Remarks.
Thomas Keegan		July 29, 1864.	At Rockville, Md.
William McMillan		" 29,	do
John Whaland		" 29,	do

September, 1864.

Returned from Desertion.

Eben Thompson		Sept. 1, 1864.	In the field.

October, 1864.

Deceased.

John H Jackson		Sept. 10, 1864.	Of disease.
John H McKeen		Oct. 19,	Killed in action.
Jeremiah Murphy		" 19,	do

SIXTH BATTERY.

August, 1864.

Deceased.

Ambrose S Lemont		Aug. 9, 1864.	In hospital.

Transferred.

Eben Reed		May —, 1864.	To V. R. Corps.

September, 1864.

No alterations.

October, 1864.

Discharged.

Thomas D Pinkham		Oct. 16, 1864.	For disability.

SEVENTH BATTERY.

August, 1864.

Deceased.

Joseph R Niles		July 26, 1864.	From wounds received in action.
Chas E Wheeler		Aug. 6,	Of disease.

September, 1864.

Discharged.

Wm R Dean		Aug. 31, 1864.	For disability.

Deceased.

Charles W Ackley		July 17, 1864.	Of disease.
Wm Andrews		Aug. 27,	do

October, 1864.

Samuel Goodwin		Oct. 4, 1864.	Of disease.

COMPANY D, SECOND U. S. SHARPSHOOTERS.

August, 1864.

Returned from Desertion.

Names.	Co.	Date.	Remarks.
John Keenan		Aug. 1, 1864.	

Deceased.

George H Coffin		Aug. 26, 1864. Of disease.	

September.

No alterations.

October, 1864.

Deceased.

Rufus H Teague		Oct. 16, 1864. Of disease.	

FIRST REGIMENT INFANTRY, (3 months.)

Organized May 4th, 1861, and mustered out August 5th, 1861, at Portland, Me., by Capt. Thomas Hight, U. S. A.

FIRST REGIMENT INFANTRY, (VET. VOLS.)

Composed of recruits and re-enlisted men of 5th, 6th and 7th Regiments of Infantry.

August, 1864.

Deserted.

W Drown	G	July 13, 1864.	At Washington, D. C.
Walter Eckhart	G	June 10,	At Petersburg.
Charles Glozier	G	Aug. 3,	At Monocacy, Md.
—— Ingersoll	G	June 10,	At Petersburg.
Peter Jolier	G	Aug. 3,	At Monocacy, Md.
J Plant	G	June 10,	At Petersburg.
A Wentworth	G	" 12,	do

Discharged.

Stillman P Getchell		Aug. 6, 1864.	For promotion.
Benj F Bicknell	C	" 8,	do

Deceased.

Warren Farrar	K		From wounds received in action.
Elden Townsend	F	July 7, 1864.	do

Missing.

John Hale	F		In action.
Adolphus W Curtis	F		do
Orrin R Messer	F		do
J Thompson	G	May 6, 1864.	do
J T Mills	G	Aug. 21,	do
F Morehouse	G	May 6,	do
Edward Sisk	G		do

FIRST REGIMENT INFANTRY, VET. VOLS., (Continued.)

SEPTEMBER, 1864.

Returned from Desertion.

Names.	Co.	Date.	Remarks.
Charles E Moody	A	Sept. 17, 1864.	In the field.

Deserted.

Freeman Ham	B	July 20, 1864.	
James Devine	F		
Joseph L Evans	I	Sept. 19,	

Discharged.

Chas H Manning	B	Sept. 8, 1864.	Time expired.
Wm McDaniel	B		For disability.
William H Savage	K	Sept. 9,	For promotion.
George T Holmes	H.Stew	" —,	By order.

Deceased.

Magloire Gosselin	D	Sept. 22, 1864.	Killed in action.
Capen W Johnson	H	Aug. 20.	From wounds received in action.
Joseph Hanneford	I		do
Amos K McLaughlin	I	Sept. 19,	Of disease.

Missing.

Frank M Smith	B	Sept. 8, 1864.	Captured by guerillas.

Returned from Missing in Action.

Asa Robbins	C	Sept. 30, 1864.	
David C Whitney	C	" 30.	
Charles W Johnson	C	" 30,	
Edmund Ladd	C	" 30,	
John George	C	" 30,	
John F Follett	G		

OCTOBER, 1864.

Returned from Desertion.

Jonathan Smith	G	Oct. 17, 1864.	

Deserted.

Thomas King	I	Oct. 6, 1864.	

Discharged.

David L Farnham	A	Oct. 8, 1864.	Time expired.
Harrison J Dwinal	B	" 7,	do
George Whitman	B	" 7,	do
Henry A Balcom	E	Sept. 27,	For disability.
John Nichols	Pr Mus	Oct. 6,	By order.
James E Holmes	"	" 6,	do

Deceased.

Horace B Chadbourne	B	Oct. 19, 1864.	Killed in action.
Abram S Brooks	A	" 19,	do
Wm A Keene	C	" 19,	do
George Sherwood	C	Sept. 23,	From wounds received in action.
Charles L Billington	E	Oct. 19,	Killed in action.
Terrence Feely	H	" 19,	do

FIRST REGIMENT INFANTRY, VET. VOLS., (Continued.)

Deceased.

Names.	Co.	Date.	Remarks.
Warren B Stinson	I	Oct. 19, 1864.	Killed in action.
James Johnson	I		From wounds received in action.
John Magner	K	Oct. 19, 1864.	Killed in action.
Geo W Conners	K	" 19,	do
Augustus S Gray	I	" 28,	Of disease.

Missing.

Harvey B Chandler	C	May 10, 1864.	Probably dead.
Charles Hanneford	H	Oct. 19,	do

Returned from Missing.

Henry H Hutchinson	A	Oct. 10, 1864.	In the field.

SECOND REGIMENT INFANTRY, (2 years.)

Mustered into U. S. service May 28, 1861, and mustered out June 4th and 9th, 1863, at Bangor, Me., by Capt. Thos. C. J. Baily, 17th U. S. Infantry.

THIRD REGIMENT INFANTRY, (3 years.)

Mustered into U. S. service, June 4th, 1861, and mustered out June 28th, 1864, at Augusta, Me., by Captain Thomas C. J. Baily. The re-enlisted men and recruits of this Regiment were transferred to the 17th Regiment Infantry Maine Volunteers.

Enlisted men mustered out with the Regiment on account of expiration of term of service.

Anson R Morrison	S. Maj.	June 28, 1864.
Thomas McFadden	Q. M.S.	do
Lorenzo W Grafton	C. Sgt.	do
John Littlefield jr	H.Stew	do
Charles Ellis	D. Maj.	do
Charles T Hooper	A	do
L Littlefield	A	do
Timothy B Curtis	A	do
Charles N Osgood	A	do
J Newcomb jr	A	do
John H Raymond	A	do
Charles T Butler	A	do
Wesley Oliver	A	do
William H Durgin	A	do
John W Adams	A	do
Lewis K Blair	A	do
Thomas J Campbell	A	do
A Cummings	A	do
John E Foley	A	do
Robert S Hatch	A	do
Henry H House	A	do
William Hughes	A	do
R F Hutchins	A	do
John A Lord	A	do
A Lemont	A	do
Charles M Morton	A	do

FIRST REGIMENT INFANTRY, 3 years, (Continued.)

Enlisted men mustered out, etc.

Names.	Co.	Date.	Remarks.
John Ridley	A	June 28, 1861.	
Fred Gannett	B	do	
Thomas O Pease	B	do	
Reuel Merrill	B	do	
Frank E Sager	B	do	
George M Bean	B	do	
Nathan H Call	B	do	
William O Clark	B	do	
Samuel A Myrick	B	do	
Benjamin Sedgerly	B	do	
W Sparks	B	do	
George H Thompson	B	do	
Joseph F Winslow	B	do	
Charles H Martin	C	do	
Charles M Landers	C	do	
Hiram W Colburn	C	do	
W Dean	C	do	
John S Dennis	C	do	
H A Fall	C	do	
S S Fall	C	do	
Charles H Foy	C	do	
William Leighton	C	do	
George T Morrill	C	do	
Joseph C Morrison	C	do	
Lyman C Neal	C	do	
Charles H Spear	C	do	
Wm H Sturtevant	C	do	
Wm H Tobey	C	do	
George M Washburn	C	do	
William Wight	C	do	
Francis Lightbody	D	do	
George Farnham	D	do	
Joseph E Purrington	D	do	
A Campbell	D	do	
Charles F Snell	D	do	
W W Goud	D	do	
L P Wildes	D	do	
Jotham S Carlton	D	do	
Isaac Durgin	D	do	
James Fletcher	D	do	
Alexander Mulligan	D	do	
Edward C Stinson	D	do	
Orlando Gould	E	do	
Thomas S Allen	E	do	
Henry C Carter	E	do	
William F Bragg	E	do	
John W Bryant	E	do	
Erastus B Burgess	E	do	
James S Choate	E	do	
Rodney Crosby	E	do	
Charles F Gilman	E	do	
Wm E Laughton	E	do	
Silas F Leighton	E	do	
William E Mathews	E	do	
Stephen M Simmons	E	do	
Seth Sweetland	E	do	
Noah F Weeks	E	do	

FIRST REGIMENT INFANTRY, 3 years, (Continued.)

Enlisted men mustered out, etc.

Names.	Co.	Date.	Remarks.
Francis H Weymouth	E	June 28, 1864.	
Ora M Nason	F	do	
George F Rich	F	do	
George W Stewart	F	do	
Charles B Russell	F	do	
M V B Judkins	F	do	
John L Fish	F	do	
John F Frost	F	do	
Benj Greenleaf	F	do	
H Hunnewell jr	F	do	
Wm J Rackliffe	F	do	
Ellis N Randall	F	do	
Henry B Swan	F	do	
Frank Swan	F	do	
Wm H Weston	F	do	
L A Williamson	F	do	
Wm E Brown	G	do	
George W Davis	G	do	
Geo C Drummond	G	do	
Chas H Selden	G	do	
Chas W Derocher	G	do	
Henry J Goulding	G	do	
L E Hodges	G	do	
John G Wiley	G	do	
Chas H Arnold	G	do	
Albert Austin	G	do	
Charles Bacon	G	do	
Chas H Buswell	G	do	
Henry Derocher	G	do	
Luther N Eames	G	do	
Henry Field	G	do	
Samuel E Frost	G	do	
C C Griffin	G	do	
William Graves	G	do	
C C Grover	G	do	
Simon Grover	G	do	
George Lashus	G	do	
S McCausland	G	do	
Joseph Morgan	G	do	
Nathaniel Perley	G	do	
Henry Pollard	G	do	
Frank D Pullen	G	do	
Hiram G Robinson	G	do	
Augustus M Sawtelle	G	do	
James A Thomas	G	do	
A Hubbard	H	do	
G W Robinson	H	do	
John F Stanley	H	do	
A B Woodman	H	do	
Henry Crowell	H	do	
Baxter Crowell	H	do	
Horace Bow	H	do	
Geo R Freeman	H	do	
I H James	H	do	
Isaac Rowe	H	do	
Charles H Stone	H	do	
John Tallus	H	do	

FIRST REGIMENT INFANTRY, 3 years, (Continued.)

Enlisted men mustered out, etc.

Names.	Co.	Date.	Remarks.
Andrew Nichols	I	June 28, 1864.	
Henry A Griffith	I	do	
Daniel Chadwick	I	do	
Frank M Boynton	I	do	
William Stover	I	do	
Cyrus B Whittier	I	do	
Wm H Spofford	I	do	
B C Bickford	I	do	
Levi W Brann	I	do	
Samuel Gowell	I	do	
Alexander Lewis	I	do	
Leonard H Livermore	I	do	
Frank S Martin	I	do	
William Maher	I	do	
John A Mann	I	do	
Rufus S McCurdy	I	do	
Geo W McDaniel	I	do	
Hezekiah Ridley	I	do	
Wm S Thoms	I	do	
Fred H Strout	K	do	
Hugh S Newell	K	do	
A P Bachelder	K	do	
A T H Wood	K	do	
Joseph T Brown	K	do	
Stephen Allen	K	do	
John W Bussell	K	do	
George A Butler	K	do	
Wm Heald	K	do	
James M Holmes	K	do	
Daniel S Norris	K	do	
Daniel W Philbrook	K	do	
James C Ricker	K	do	
Patrick H Snell	K	do	
Joseph H Stearns	K	do	
Henry S Turner	K	do	
Wm O Wilson	K	do	

FOURTH REGIMENT INFANTRY, (3 years.)

Mustered into U. S. service June 15th, 1861, and mustered out at Rockland, Me., on the 19th day of July, 1864, by Capt. Thomas C. J. Baily, 17th U. S. Infantry. The re-enlisted men and recruits of this Regiment were transferred to the 19th Regiment Maine Volunteers.

Enlisted men mustered out with the Regiment on account of expiration of term of service.

Wm H Gardiner	S. Maj.	July 19, 1864.	
Henry C Tibbetts	Q.M.S.	do	
Samuel S Hersey	H Stew	do	
John F Singhi	P.Mus.	do	
Fred A Alders	A	do	
Thomas H Gurney	A	do	
Henry W Ladd	A	do	
Tolford Dunham	A	do	
Joseph P Libby	A	do	

4

FOURTH REGIMENT INFANTRY, 3 years, (Continued.)

Enlisted men mustered out, etc.

Names.	Co.	Date.	Remarks.
Jerry Denning	A	July 19, 1864.	
James Gall	A	do	
Horace Speed	A	do	
Wm H Clifford	A	do	
Eben M Sanborn	A	do	
E F Allenwood	A	do	
D J Bryant	A	do	
Melvin Cooley	A	do	'
William Cullnan	A	do	
Stephen O Curtis	A	do	
George S Daniels	A	do	
Otis A Dickey	A	do	
Daniel D Flye	A	do	
Henry C Hall	A	do	
Enos M Hatch	A	do	
H C Heal	A	do	
M Law	A	do	
A S Lord	A	do	
M Nichols	A	do	
B F Philbrick	A	do	
A Piper	A	do	
Geo A Russ	A	do	
John B Smith	A	do	
Dennis Sweeney	A	do	
Anson T Trussell	A	do	
Thomas Wentworth	A	de	
James B Walker	A	do	
Havilah Pease	B	do	
E L Mowry	B	do	
T S Pillsbury	B	do	
W W Ulmer	B	do	
John B Lougy	B	do	
Robert Grant	B	do	
George E Hall	B	do	
Charles E Gove	B	do	
Ellis Bigdoll	B	do	
M A Blackington	B	do	
James W Clark	B	do	
John M Doe	B	do	
D Y Dow	B	do	
H J Dow	B	do	
Geo H Dunbar	B	do	
A J Gardiner	B	do	
Albert Goodwin	B	do	
John J Kellock	B	do	
Albion K Prentiss	B	do	
Josiah C Spear	B	do	
Geo F Stetson	B	do	
Geo H Tighe	B	do	
John W Titus	B	do	
Samuel S Totman	B	do	
Aruna Willis	B	do	
Alden F Wooster	B	do	
John H Young	C	do	
John Colburn	C	do	
Alfred W Cunningham	C	do	
James Balkomb	C	do	

FOURTH REGIMENT INFANTRY, 3 years, (Continued.)

Enlisted men mustered out, etc.

Names.	Co.	Date.	Remarks.
J M Brown	C	July 19, 1864.	
O F Brown	C	do	
E K Butler	C	do	
Horatio G Collins	C	do	
Alden Crockett	C	do	
Patrick Martin	C	do	
N C Matthews	C	do	
Benj F Palmer	C	do	
Charles C Perry	C	do	
Andrew Pottle	C	do	
C J Ramsey	C	do	
Rufus Robbins	C	do	
George Sheldon	C	do	
Albert Shepherd	C	do	
Geo A Staples	C	do	
Walter Sutherland	C	do	
John H Thomas	C	do	
James F Tuttle	C	do	
John F Walker	C	do	
Benj F Walter	C	do	
Joshua G Whitney	C	do	
Jacob Winslow	C	do	
James McLaughlin	D	do	
Allen P Farrington	D	do	
Mark Perry	D	do	
William Fountain	D	do	
L G Perry	D	do	
H O Davis	D	do	
Thomas Kelly	D	do	
Eben E Pusher	D	do	
William Perkins	D	do	
Charles P Burns	D	do	
John R Chase	D	do	
Elias Davis	D	do	
Isaiah V Eaton	D	do	
A Fields	D	do	
James Hatch	D	do	
Charles Hodges	D	do	
Elward H Joy	D	do	
H Marshall	D	do	
Christopher Martin	D	do	
A J Millay	D	do	
John Miller	D	do	
John Morrissey	D	do	
George Peasley	D	do	.
Horatio Richards	D	do	
Lafayette Richards	D	do	
Appleton Townsend	D	do	
Jerome Watson	D	do	
Nathaniel B Waters	E	do	
Ira A Waltz	E	do	
Frank H Lailer	E	do	
Charles K Chapman	E	do	
Everett B Chapman	E	do	
E Coombs	E	do	
S N Fales	E	do	
I W Fountain	E	do	

FOURTH REGIMENT INFANTRY, 3 years, (Continued.)

Enlisted men mustered out, etc.

Names.	Co.	Date.	Remarks.
Daniel E Gammage	E	July 19, 1864.	
Oscar C Gove	E	do	
W W Gove	E	do	
Almond Hall	E	do	
H M Hall	E	do	
J H Hodgkins	E	do	
J S Kinney	E	do	
Frank Morang	E	do	
Geo D Osgood	E	do	
H C Plummer	E	do	
S G Sidelinger	E	do	
Evander G Snow	E	do	
John R Skinner	E	do	
John L Thompson	E	do	
Charles C Turner	E	do	
Lucius B Varney	E	do	
Isaac T Waters	E	do	
Albert H Rose	F	do	
Henry Leach	F	do	
F O J S Hill	F	do	
Hiram G York	F	do	
Joseph G Hilt	F	do	
Charles B Parsons	F	do	
W H Chick	F	do	
F M Roberts	F	do	
R G Bickford	F	do	
John F Stone	F	do	
Henry A Colagin	F	do	
M L Knowlton	F	do	
E J Barlow	F	do	
Edward H Bean	F	do	
J H Bickford	F	do	
Emerson Cilley	F	do	
A D Crocker	F	do	
Amos Evans	F	do	
Francis M Forbes	F	do	
John H Gardiner	F	do	
Harrison Hall	F	do	
James H Hines	F	do	
D C Nickerson	F	do	
N R Nelson	F	do	
Nathan Patterson	F	do	
Daniel Pierce jr	F	do	
John A Poland	F	do	
Enoch F Piper	F	do	
Frank Rowe jr	F	do	
Chas H Rowell	F	do	
E D Tasker	F	do	
Robert Waterman jr	F	do	
Thomas O Whitcomb	F	do	
John G Somes	G	do	
Daniel O Howard	G	do	
George Tibbetts	G	do	
Alexander Nute	G	do	
Augustus H Cookson	G	do	
John Downey	G	do	
Fairfield Erskine	G	do	

FOURTH REGIMENT INFANTRY, 3 years, (Continued.)

Enlisted men mustered out, etc.

Names.	Co	Date.	Remarks.
Peter Fredson jr	G	July 19, 1864.	
A C Lowell	G	do	
David G Munsey	G	do	
William Munsey	G	do	
John H Thomas	H	do	
Horace C Clough	H	do	
Levi Roberts	H	do	
George L Ames	H	do	
Alfred Blackington	H	do	
John Butler	H	do	
Alvin K Jameson	H	do	
John Keefe	H	do	
Stillman Mink	H	do	
Isaac Stahl	H	do	
Harrison Simmons	H	do	
Alexander M Wallace	H	do	
Clement H Stevens	I	do	
Elias B Moore	I	do	
Moses H Witham	I	do	
L E Pendleton	I	do	
R G Ames	I	do	
I W Baird	I	do	
David Blanchard	I	do	
H D Calderwood	I	do	
M C Clark	I	do	
Oscar F Colson	I	do	
John C Fowler	I	do	
Charles P Parker	I	do	
Geo W Patterson	I	do	
Chas A Phinney	I	do	
O P Seidlinger	I	do	
R P Seidlinger	I	do	
Wm S Towers	I	do	
John Ward	I	do	
Clifton Whittam	I	do	
James E Doak	K	do	
Sears Nickerson	K	do	
S M Perkins	K	do	
Elisha Hanning	K	do	
Dennis Moody	K	do	
Eleazer J Young	K	do	
Benj F Young	K	do	
Clinton C Collins	K	do	
Geo L Feyler	K	do	
Andrew Herrin	K	do	
Samuel Jackson	K	do	
Isaiah B Merrick	K	do	
H M A Poor	K	do	
Jacob D Ray	K	do	
John A Rines	K	do	
John A Robinson	K	do	
Robert Whitehead	K	do	

FIFTH REGIMENT INFANTRY, (3 years.)

Mustered into U. S. service June 24, 1861, and mustered out on the 27th day of July, 1864, at Portland, Me., by Lieut. I. H. Walker, 14th U. S. Infantry. The recruits and re-enlisted men of this Regiment were transferred and organized as the 1st Regiment Infantry, Veteran Volunteers.

Enlisted men mustered out with the Regiment on account of expiration of term of service.

Names.	Co.	Date.	Remarks.
James L Dresser	C. Sgt.	July 27, 1864.	
Orrin G Pratt	H.Stew	do	
John L Haskell	A	do	
O W Rogers	A	do	
R Edwards	A	do	
C M Edwards	A	do	
David C Crockett	A	do	
Theodore Shackford	A	do	
A J Stackpole	A	do	
Chas H Stuart	A	do	
Oliver Cilley	A	do	•
W H Farwell	A	do	
A E Foss	A	do	
Fred Hill	A	do	
F E Henley	A	do	
Levi Hall	A	do	
Alfred O Lowell	A	do	
Isaac Linscott	A	do	
E B Phinney	A	do	
James G Spaulding	A	do	
C C Shaw	A	do	
Cyrus S Libby	A	do	
Moses M Staples	A	do	
Alvin V Tufts	A	do	
John F Linscott	B	do	
Samuel B Brackett	B	do	
Timothy Elliott	B	do	
James Stevens	B	do	
Thomas Heney	B	do	
Fred B Nesbitt	B	do	
Oliver B Adams	B	do	
Jesse W Adams	B	do	
Thomas W Applebee	B	do	
Chas H Brown	B	do	
A H Bean	B	do	
P M Cousins	B	do	
H A Dearborn	B	do	
Joseph Elliott	B	do	
Chas P Foster	B	do	
S F Goodwin	B	do	
John Harper	B	do	
Jesse Jeffries	B	do	
Charles O Libby	B	do	
C F Larrabee	B	do	
John E Moran	B	do	
H P Smith	B	do	
William Stevens	B	do	
Jere Sullivan	B	do	
Benj F Leavitt	C	do	
Martin Hughes	C	do	
Wm W Sawyer	C	do	

FIFTH REGIMENT INFANTRY, 3 years, (Continued.)

Enlisted men mustered out, etc.

Names.	Co.	Date.	Remarks.
Sylvester S Wormwell	C	July 27, 1864.	
Eli Dennett	C	do	
James D Deas	C	do	
Dexter Avery	C	do	
Wm H Atkinson	C	do	
George H Andrews	C	do	
Joseph Bell	C	do	
Josiah C Bassick	C	do	
John Cilley	C	do	
Alonzo Cole	C	do	
Milton J King	C	do	
Luther G Kimball	C	do	
Geo F Morgan	C	do	
James O Patrick	C	do	
Charles Ricker	C	do	
Frank Ricker	C	do	
James Senate	C	do	
Thomas B Stone	C	do	
Chas H P Stevens	C	do	
Michael Thyne	C	do	
Joseph Wilbur	C	do	
Benj F Whitten	C	do	
John H Willard	C	do	
Leonard Welch	C	do	
Samuel Wentworth	C	do	
Alonzo Haley	D	do	
Wm C Moody	D	do	
James T Crowell	D	do	
S L Johnson	D	do	
Ai C Harrington	D	do	
Henry W Farrow	D	do	
D Whitney	D	do	
John Willis	D	do	
Chas E Marriner	D	do	
R T Alexander	D	do	
Geo L Colby	D	do	
John Colby	D	do	
Edwin Cobb	D	do	
C A Clough	D	do	
John Conley	D	do	
O Dunning	D	do	
O Eastman	D	do	
Anthony Fabian	D	do	
Robert Few	D	do	
Lorenzo D Fox	D	do	
James E Howland	D	do	
Wm H Hanilin	D	do	
Geo L Harmon	D	do	
Laurence Hassett	D	do	
William Labee	D	do	
Stephen Perkins	D	do	
Thomas Steward	D	do	
Albion Slowman	D	do	
Israel C Somers	D	do	
Albert Vickery	D	do	
Chas B Vickery	D	do	
M Welch	D	do	

FIFTH REGIMENT INFANTRY, 3 years, (Continued.)

Enlisted men mustered out, etc.

Names.	Co.	Date.	Remarks.
Jerry Warren	D	July 27, 1864.	
Norris Litchfield	E	do	
Henry Murphy	E	do	
Francis Day	E	do	
Ephraim Litchfield	E	do	
John Casey	E	do	
Harrison Carpenter	E	do	
Henry J Estes	E	do	
Clifton Jones	E	do	
Horace E Kimball	E	do	
Luther Litchfield	E	do	
Lucius L Lothrop	E	do	
John L Verrill	E	do	
Isaac C Yeaton	E	do	
Llewellyn Goodwin	F	do	
Daniel Y Gallison	F	do	
Frank C Kimball	F	do	
Lincoln Gower	F	do	
James Fitzsimmons	F	do	
William Hayes	F	do	
Peter Kelly	F	do	
John McDonald	F	do	
Hiram H Ricker	F	do	
John Timmony	F	do	
William Tobey	F	do	
Chas G Hall	G	do	
Alonzo Mitchell	G	do	
Jeremiah C Kenniston	G	do	
Stephen C Stanford	G	do	
James Blake	G	do	
James Brown	G	do	
Charles H Chick	G	do	
Edward L Clark	G	do	
Philip Drinkwater	G	do	
Elvin L Hamlin	G	do	
Chas H Jordan	G	do	
Isaac N Jackson	G	do	
James Killeen	G	do	
Timothy Kelley	G	do	
Hillman Saunders	G	do	
Wm S S Welch	G	do	
Benj P Wentworth	G	do	
Chas H Dow	H	do	
James G Sanborn	H	do	
Wm N True	H	do	
Geo W Tappan	H	do	
Anthony B Gould	H	do	
John Burnes	H	do	
Geo W Briggs	H	do	
James Conlin	H	do	
Thos R Chase	H	do	
Wm Goodness	H	do	
George W Holmes	H	do	
Geo N Maxham	H	do	
Leudall R Newell	H	do	
Geo B Sturgis	H	do	
Otis H Skillings	H	do	

FIFTH REGIMENT INFANTRY, 3 years, (Continued.)

Enlisted men mustered out, etc.

Names.	Co.	Date.	Remarks.
George F True	H	July 27, 1864.	
William Tracey	H	do	
Enoch Whittemore jr	I	do	
Bethuel S Sawyer	I	do	
Andrew J Bean	I	do	
Cyrus R Lawrence	I	do	
John F Bean	I	do	
W R York	I	do	
H K Chase	I	do	
Charles W Horne	I	do	
Robert Howe	I	do	
Wm R Harper	I	do	
Asa D Jordan	I	do	
James Kelley	I	do	
S N Littlehale	I	do	
Lorenzo D Russell	I	do	
Chas M Wentworth	I	do	
Geo W Pratt	K	do	
Ellis Ripley	K	do	
Richard Bailey	K	do	
Stephen M Barrows	K	do	
John F Bincroft	K	do	
Ezra M Goodwin	K	do	
Samuel H Hutchins	K	do	
Charles F McKenney	K	do	
John Meserve	K	do	
Marshall S Phillips	K	do	
Chas A Richardson	K	do	
Joshua S Spiller	K	do	
Alanson W St Clair	K	do	
Horace A Verrill	K	do	

SIXTH REGIMENT INFANTRY, (3 years.)

Mustered into U. S. service July 15th, 1861, and mustered out August 15th, 1864, at Portland, by Lieut. I. H. Walker, 14th U. S. Infantry. The re-enlisted men and recruits of this Regiment were transferred and organized into the 1st Regiment Infantry, Veteran Volunteers.

Enlisted men mustered out with the Regiment on account of expiration of term of service.

Wm H West	S. Maj. Aug.	15, 1864.	do
Geo H Snowman	C. Sgt.	do	do
Thomas J Rockwell	A	do	do
John B Bates jr	A	do	do
L Berry	A	do	do
Henry K White	A	do	do
Newton Blanchard	A	do	do
Alphonzo Bradley	A	do	do
Albert L Bragg	A	do	do
Levi Bagley	A	do	do
Seth B Crockett	A	do	do
E T Crockett	A	do	do
O W Fox	A	do	do
Benjamin Harris	A	do	do

5

SIXTH REGIMENT INFANTRY, 3 years, (Continued.)
Enlisted men mustered out, etc.

Names.	Co.	Date.	Remarks.
F G Pratt	A	Aug. 15, 1864.	
Henry Ricker jr	A	do	
Alexander M Robinson	A	do	
Andrew J Robinson jr	A	do	
Timothy Wetherbee	A	do	
Wm G Sewall	A	do	
Chas H Whittemore	A	do	
Geo F Peaks	B	do	
David Clark	B	do	
S S Boynton	B	do	
Edward B Cook	B	do	
John H Christy	B	do	
Thomas Corrigan	B	do	
B S Foster	B	do	
William George	B	do	
H S George	B	do	
Jesse F Hines	B	do	
A Hunt	B	do	
J R Jewell	B	do	
J A Joy	B	do	
Billings Maddox	B	do	
Roscoe G Taylor	B	do	
Wm D Thompson	B	do	
Augustus J Trueworthy	B	do	
C A Treworgy	B	do	
David A West	B	do	
B A Campbell	C	do	
Wm H McCabe	C	do	
A H Campbell	C	do	
B R Thaxter	C	do	
Theodore Hill jr	C	do	
Samuel O Bryant	C	do	
Wm K Stiles	C	do	
Geo H Allen	C	do	
H H Bowles	C	do	
James Black	C	do	
Thomas Conniff	C	do	
James E Crane	C	do	
Gilbert L Edgecomb	C	do	
Jeremiah Hennessy	C	do	
E L Hitchings	C	do	
James N Lyon	C	do	
David Millay	C	do	
John Perry	C	do	
Wm N Gower	D	do	
John Chamberlain	D	do	
Alonzo Smith	D	do	
Thomas Mahoney	D	do	
Elias Smith	D	do	
Henry Swarbrick	D	do	
Horace C Wilson	D	do	
James Stubbs jr	E	do	
Waldo S Richards	E	do	
Stephen B Wescott	E	do	
John M Rice	E	do	
Sewall L Heyward	E	do	
George W Clay	E	do	

SIXTH REGIMENT INFANTRY, 3 years, (Continued.)

Enlisted men mustered out, etc.

Names.	Co.	Date.	Remarks.
Lewis P Abbott	E	Aug. 15, 1864.	
Edward L Colson	E	do	
John Carroll	E	do	
A H Carter	E	do	
Charles L Davis	E	do	
Charles H Doak	E	do	
Francis J Dudley	E	do	
Albert N Eaton	E	do	
John Keefe	E	do	
Edward D Lampher	E	do	
Chales A Pillsbury	E	do	
Arthur I Saunders	E	do	
J Towle jr	E	do	
Justin H Trundy	E	do	
Wm H Lincoln	F	do	
James R Hayward	F	do	
Thomas Mathewson	F	do	
Reuben N Maker	F	do	
Joseph Gilmore	F	do	
Simeon A Spofford	F	do	
Charles H Bailey	F	do	
Freeman F Dudley	F	do	
Isaac Gardner	F	do	
William Kelley	F	do	
Thomas Moran	F	do	
John W Reynolds	F	do	
John Redman	F	do	
Albert Sawtelle	F	do	
Amos Ward	F	do	
Thomas Welch	F	do	
Matthew Wood	F	do	
Charles Frye	G	do	
G Leighton	G	do	
George H Peva	G	do	
Samuel C Chase	G	do	
Joseph Robinette	G	do	
Robert Bailey	G	do	
Robert Dixon	G	do	
Michael McLaughlin	G	do	
Charles W McGregor	G	do	
Gilbert McKinnon	G	do	
Thomas O'Brien	G	do	
John E Stewart	G	do	
Alonzo Y Stevens	G	do	
H S Tibbetts	G	do	
Elisha Eddy	H	do	
David B Herrick	H	do	
Lendall H Whittier	H	do	
Joseph F Getchell	H	do	
Charles F Tibbetts	H	do	
Evans Beale	H	do	
Joseph Bulger	H	do	
Charles Chase	H	do	
George H Cooley	H	do	
O D Chapman	H	do	
Charles Fitzgerald	H	do	
Joseph S Hammond	H	do	

SIXTH REGIMENT INFANTRY, 3 years, (Continued.)

Enlisted men mustered out, etc.

Names.	Co.	Date.	Remarks.
Harrison T Norton	H	Aug. 15, 1864.	
Erasmus E Page	H	do	
James H Roundy	H	do	
Upton T Smith	H	do	
William H Sewall	H	do	
James S Knowlton	I	do	
Arthur P Benner	I	do	
William H Brown	I	do	
Martin V Gilmore	I	do	
Oscar E W Hinckley	I	do	
Hezekiah F Harris	I	do	
George W House	I	do	
James A Lane	I	do	
Thomas McCallum	I	do	
Nathaniel P Randall	I	do	
George W Sleeper	I	do	
Thomas B Sturtivant	I	do	
Thatcher Vose	K	do	
Levi Flood	K	do	
George Anderson	K	do	
Alonzo F Foster	K	do	
John Bryan	K	do	
Daniel W Bagley	K	do	
Peter Chester	K	do	
James H Dingee	K	do	
C N Drew	K	do	
Geo M Dyer	K	do	
Jacob S Hinckley	K	do	
F Potter	K	do	
Jeremiah Pike	K	do	
Josiah Roberts	K	do	
Samuel L Smith	K	do	
S W Seeley	K	do	
Thomas J Saddler	K	do	
Allen Ure	K	do	

SEVENTH REGIMENT INFANTRY, (3 years.)

Mustered into U. S. service August 21st, 1861, and mustered out at Augusta, Me., September 5, 1864, by Capt. C. Holmes, U. S. A. The re-enlisted men and recruits of this Regiment were re-organized into the 1st Regiment Infantry, Veteran Volunteers, together with those transferred from the 5th and 6th Regiments Infantry.

Enlisted men mustered out with the Regiment on account of expiration of term of service.

F L Richards	C. Sgt.	Sept. 5, 1864.
Xantheus A Withee	B	do
Seward Merrill	B	do
Wm B Parker	B	do
Eli McLaughlin	C	do
Moses W McKay	C	do
Alvin E True	C	do
Josiah Baker	C	do
Josiah Barker	C	do
Thomas Fish	C	do

SEVENTH REGIMENT INFANTRY, 3 years, (Continued.)

Enlisted men mustered out, &c.

Names.	Co.	Date.	Remarks.
Frank O Hanscomb	C	Sept. 5, 1864.	
Andrew J Hatch	C	do	
William Kennedy	C	do	
Benj W Mitchell	C	do	
Joseph Moreau	C	do	
Adrian E Turner	C	do	
Alfred A Stevens	D	do	
Flavel H Goodwin	D	do	
Joseph F Call	D	do	
George D Webb	D	do	
William Barrows	D	do	
Charles Bennett	D	do	
Silas Crooker	D	do	
Geo F Coolbroth	D	do	
L C Dillingham	D	do	
Geo W Haskell	D	do	
James Lewin	D	do	
Thomas B Powers	D	do	
Thos A Richardson	D	do	
Horace Ross	D	do	
William Smith	D	do	
Lewis L Thurston	D	do	
Chas H Rounds	D	do	
James D Williams	D	do	
Chas W Smiley	E	do	
N S Burrill	E	do	
James H Jacobs	E	do	
Chas A Waterhouse	F	do	
Edwin Bradbury	F	do	
Wm T Trundy	F	do	
Samuel Young	F	do	
John E Proctor	G	do	
Reuel N Fields	G	do	
William Hudson	G	do	
Thomas B Rose	I	do	
Henry H Cook	I	do	
Hiram Baker	I	do	
Charles Clarke	I	do	
Julius C Chandler	I	do	
Edward Conlin	I	do	
Edward F Garland	I	do	
Jeremiah Getchell	I	do	
Stephen McNeal	I	do	
Newell Pomeroy	I	do	
Allien Crockett	K	do	
A K Chase	K	do	
Jabez B Eveleth	K	do	
Bradford Howard	K	do	
Thomas Melody	K	do	
Melville Marshal	K	do	
Osgood D Mason	K	do	
Albert M Rose	K	do	
Emerson Turner	K	do	
Albert B Thibodeau	K	do	
Spencer Wadsworth	K	do	
Gardner Waterhouse	K	do	
Joseph F Williams	K	do	

EIGHTH REGIMENT INFANTRY.

August, 1864.

Discharged.

Names.	Co.	Date.	Remarks.
S C Smith	I	July 31, 1864.	For disability.
Ephraim W Wiley	H	" 19,	For promotion.

Deceased.

F Sinclair	B	July 1, 1864.	
E Sanford	C	Aug. 14,	
A P Walker	D	" 1,	
T A McGrath	D	" 10,	
W M Pinkham	D	" 13,	
S A Wilson	E	June 14,	
George Robinson	G	July 30,	
T Walsh	G	" 17,	
F I Frazier	G	" 17,	
J E Cochran	G	Aug. 9,	
W C Bowley	H	July 3,	
A Prescott	H	Aug. 11,	
A P Vickery	H	July 4,	
A Pierce	H	June 27,	

Missing.

J E Russell	E	Aug. 28, 1864.	While on picket.
B Webber	E	" 28,	do

September, 1864.

Deserted.

George W Bowden	G	Aug. 8, 1864.	At Cold Harbor, Va.

Discharged.

Elijah Weaver	B	Sept. 14, 1864.	Time expired.
Edward Shurtliff	C	" 21,	do
S C Brown	E	" 15,	do
Joseph Pollard	G	" 15,	do
Albert O Bills	H	" 16,	For disability.
Samuel Woodman	F	" 10,	do
Albert F Keyes	A	" 8,	For promotion.
Moses R Adams	A	" 16,	Time expired.
John S Bean	A	do	do
Henry T Allen	A	do	do
Jason Allen	A	do	do
Nathan Pulsifer	A	do	do
Algernon U Mitchell	A	do	do
Wm W Leavitt	A	do	do
Abraham T Taylor	A	do	do
Geo B Adams	A	do	do
Nelson W Adams	A	do	do
Samuel Gilman	A	do	do
Leonard H Pickens	A	do	do
Wm H Linscott	A	do	do
Erasmus B Woodard	A	do	do
Geo W Emery	B	do	do
Roscoe Cram	B	do	do
Lewis Clement	B	do	do
Randall Gallison	B	do	do

EIGHTH REGIMENT INFANTRY, (Continued.)
Discharged.

Names.	Co.	Date.	Remarks.
Charles E Higgins	B	Sept. 16, 1864.	Time expired.
James B Ingalls	B	do	do
Wm M Jameson	B	do	do
A Kimball	B	do	do
Geo W Hilton	B	do	do
Frank M Pinkham	B	do	do
Josiah Libby	C	do	do
L S Chase	C	do	do
Sylvester Graves	C	do	do
Wm F Linnell	C	do	do
S L Delano	C	do	do
E L Gordon	C	do	do
William A Cole	C	do	do
Hiram Martin	D	do	do
Adolphus Niles	D	do	do
David L Boyle	D	do	do
Moses Atkinson	D	do	do
Chas M Stafford	D	do	do
John O Perry	D	do	do
George Woods	D	do	do
Chauncey B Webster	E	do	do
James M Pote	E	do	do
Silas R Brown	E	do	do
Charles L Davis	E	do	do
John Gould	E	do	do
George Paine	E	do	do
Nathan W Savage	E	do	do
Samuel Cole	F	do	do
H A Henderson	F	do	do
J P Reynolds	F	do	do
A W Fox	F	do	do
Thomas Seavey	F	do	do
A P Downs	F	do	do
J S Hersom	F	do	do
J S Getchell	F	do	do
Joseph C Gray	G	do	do
Peter Collins	G	do	do
George S Ingalls	G	do	do
Lewis Lacey	G	do	do
Albert Daggett	H	do	do
H rce P Packard	H	do	do
Thomas Butler	I	do	do
Jam s Pusty	I	do	do
Walter H Morrison	I	do	do
G tt Luther	I	do	do
Orlando Staples	I	do	do
Elliet Robinson	I	do	do
M s Roper	I	do	do
Benjamin Lamson	K	do	do
James Sawyer	K	do	do
W H Folsom	K	do	do
Edward Storer	K	do	do
Rodney Sutton	K	la	do
John A Spaulding	K	do	do
Isaac Myers	K	do	do
William E ereon	K	do	do
Edward Spearin	K	do	do
Augustus B Taylor	H.Stew	do	do

EIGHTH REGIMENT INFANTRY, (Continued.)

Deceased.

Names.	Co.	Date.	Remarks.
J B Gilman	A	July 5, 1864.	From wounds received in action.
D T Stevens	A	" 26,	do
M L Withington	A	" 31,	do
W D Lewis	A	Aug. 26,	do
E N Mosher	A	July 4,	Of disease.
C G Hanley	A	June 2,	do
D Goodwin	A	Aug. 7,	do
W H Berry	D	" 28,	do
C F Atkins	D	June 25,	do
John Waite	E	Sept. 12,	do
Reuben Jones	F	Aug. 21,	do
Simeon Coffin	F	" 8,	From wounds received in action.
Chas H Orcutt	G	" 27,	Of disease.
James Sullivan	I	Sept. 8,	do
R W Witham	K	" 1,	do
—— Bubier	K	Aug. 1,	From wounds received in action.

Transferred.

A Littlefield	A	June 9, 1864.	To U. S. Navy.
J McFarland	A	" 9,	do

Returned from Missing in Action.

Mathaniel Marden	A		Erroneously dr. as missing in action.
John Scribner	A		do
A F Hardy	A		do
Ezra P Foster	A		do
Arthur T Robinson	B		do
Erastus Doble	B		do
Thomas Moreland	B		do
Chas W Moore	B		do
Wallace Smith	C		do
D Young	C		do
Geo W Bean	C		do
Lyman Maxwell	E		do
Benjamin Webber	E		do
J E Russell	E		do
Sylvester Hatch	F		do
George Rowe	F		do
W P Rankins	F	Sept. 16, 1864.	do
G S Gray	F	do	do
C H Edgcomb	F	do	do
L L Stewart	F	do	do
M T Goodwin	F	do	do
Horace Jenkins	F	do	do
O Blaisdell	F	do	do
C W Quimby	F	do	do
E T McFarland	G	do	do
J Brown	G	do	do
G Higgins	G	do	do
J Downs	G	do	do
T Doherty	G	do	do
R H Giles	G	do	do
S Griffiths	G	do	do
D Early	G	do	do
A Eaton	G	do	do
J K Richardson	G	do	do

EIGHTH REGIMENT INFANTRY, (Continued.)

Returned from Missing in Action.

Names.	Co.	Date.	Remarks.
C L Stewart	G	Sept. 16, 1864.	Erroneously dr. as missing in action.
M H Whitney	G	do	do
W Hall	H	do	do
H H Mann	H	do	do
O Metcalf	H	do	do
Wm N Norris	I	do	do
J W Young	I	do	do
H L Burnett	I	do	do
D Larrabee	I	do	do

OCTOBER, 1864.

Discharged.

H A B Keyes	A	Sept. 25, 1864.	For disability.
M Woodcock	A	" 25,	do
Richard Tinker	E	Oct. 5,	do
Seth H Hall	E	" —,	do
John Trainer	G	" 10,	do
Edward Overlock	H	Sept. 15,	do
Leonard H Evans	I	Oct. 17,	do
Oliver Yeaton	F	" —,	Time expired.
Samuel Woodman	F	" —,	For disability.
Abijah Fletcher	G	Sept. 28,	Time expired.

Deceased.

Nelson J Damnion	A	Oct. 27, 1864.	At Fair Oaks, Va.
Benj F Belcher	C	July 11,	U. S. Monitor.
Joseph M Nash	C	Sept. 4,	U. S. General Hospital.
L O Goff	C	Oct. 23,	do
D K Green	C	" 27,	At Fair Oaks, Va.
George Wheeler	D	Sept. 22,	At Fortress Monroe.
Andrew Irving	G	Oct. 3,	From wounds received in action.
Adam Eaton	G	June 18,	do
R H Giles	G	May 16,	do
Geore L Stewart	G	" 16,	do
George Wasgatt	H	Oct. 27,	At Fair Oaks, Va.
S Pinkney	I	" 11,	At Point of Rocks, Va.

NINTH REGIMENT INFANTRY.

AUGUST, 1864.

Deserted.
Daniel Murray	F	Aug. 21, 1864.	While on picket.

Discharged.
Robert Page	H	Aug. 11, 1864.	By order war department.

Deceased.
Wm H Simpson	A	Aug. 7, 1864.	From wounds received in action.
Daniel Colnaine	A	" 7,	do
John Slater	A	" 5,	Accidentally shot.
Fred A Crafts	A	June 22,	Of disease.

NINTH REGIMENT INFANTRY, (Continued.)

Deceased.

Names.	Co.	Date.	Remarks.
Gilmore P Rook	B	July 31, 1864	From wounds received in action.
Daniel Fletcher	B	Aug. 2,	Of disease.
Wm H Hutchins	B	" 3,	do
Edwin C Bates	C	" 12,	do
Loring J Beal	D	" 1,	Sun stroke.
A Town	D	July 25,	From wounds received in action.
Geo O Newbury	E	" 14,	do
Samuel Michaels	E	Aug. 4,	do
Henry A Pierce	E	" 18,	do
Freeman Murray	E	" 18,	Killed in action.
Orrin G Straw	F	" 16,	do
Louis C Bartlett	F	" 19,	Of disease.
Nathan Badger	G	July 25,	From wounds received in action.
Eben Fish	G	June 14,	do
James Geary	G	Aug. 16,	Killed in action.
Geo H Greenlief	G	June 14,	From wounds received in action.
Geo T Spraggs	G	July 5,	do
Ephraim E York	H	Aug. 16,	Killed in action.
Edward H Day	I	" 3,	From wounds received in action.
John Williams	I	" 16,	Killed in action.
Thomas K Holt	K	" 11,	From wounds received in action.
Lafayette Bray	K	" 6,	do
Frank Morton	K	" 9,	do
Luke Kenney	K	" 16,	do

Missing.

Chas B York	C	Aug. 18, 1864.	In action at Deep Run, Va.
Edward Grant	C	" 18,	do
George Dearborn	C	" 18,	do
Orlando Sawtelle	D	" 16,	do
Chas C Baker	D	" 16,	do
Chas M Harding	D	" 16,	do
A H Libby	D	" 16,	do
Cornelius Stinchfield	D	" 16,	do
Geo W Harris	G	" 18,	do
J Foley	G	" 18,	do
Timothy Mahony	K	" 16,	do

Returned from Missing in Action.

Dennis M Hogan	B	Aug. 30, 1864.	Near Petersburg, Va.
John H Wright	I	" 30,	do

SEPTEMBER, 1864.

Deserted.

Leonard Baker	K	Sept. 7, 1864.	In Maine, while on furlough.
James A Carleton	A	" 5,	do
Albert H Hunter	F	" 5,	do
Joshua O Roix	H	" 5,	do

Discharged.—Time Expired.

Edward L Brackett	C. Sgt.	Sept. 27, 1864.	
Bernard McGraw	A	do	
John W Morse	A	do	
Joseph Kidder	A	do	
Howard T Wharff	A	do	

NINTH REGIMENT INFANTRY, (Continued.)

Discharged.—Time Expired.

Names.	Co.	Date.	Remarks.
Daniel A Smith	A	Sept. 27, 1864.	
Thomas H McGraw	A	do	
Michael Barry	A	do	
James Berry	A	do	
William Ferrill	A	do	
Alexander Hill	A	do	
Warren Munson	A	do	
Abram Banco	A	do	
David E Coombs	B	do	
Samuel L Silley	B	do	
Alden O Rogers	B	do	
Robert D Hunter	B	do	
Richard B Lowell	B	do	
Joseph H Durgin	B	do	
Alonzo J Moody	B	do	
Cyrus C Randall	B	do	
Milton B Robbins	B	do	
James H Lowell	B	do	
Joseph Avery	B	do	
James H Bennett	B	do	
Emery Berry	B	do	
Wm O Blackman	B	do	
Cornelius Colby	B	do	
Woodman Crooker	B	do	
Roswell Dunton	B	do	
Wm E Freeman	B	do	
James F Goss	B	do	
C M Harris	B	do	
Fred B Haskell	B	do	
Wiles O Hunter	B	do	
Asa W Jaquith	B	do	
Phineas Leach	B	do	
John Lowell	B	do	
Granville A Preble	B	do	
Randall Rogers	B	do	
Thomas Ross	B	do	
P M Thayer	B	do	
Jacob Wilson	B	do	
Chas D York	B	do	
Richard Hussey	C	do	
John H Larrabee	C	do	
Josiah Wright	C	do	
James Witham	C	do	
Geo F Bachelder	C	do	
C F Cox	C	do	
Charles Curtis	C	do	
George Ingraham	C	do	
David Macumber	C	do	
Asa G Merrill	C	do	
John Parker	C	do	
Silas Reed	C	do	
Stephen H Mosher	D	do	
Amos Q Folsom	D	do	
Mark Haley	D	do	
John W Keene	D	do	
A McIntyre	D	do	
W Mosher	D	do	

NINTH REGIMENT INFANTRY, (Continued.)

Discharged.—Time Expired.

Names.	Co.	Date.	Remarks.
Leonard J Stafford	D	Sept. 27, 1864.	
James H Wood	D	do	
Robert Bunker	D	do	
Stephen H Day	D	do	
John W Dinsmore	D	do	
Eugene F Goodrich	D	do	
John McKinley	D	do	
Franklin B Nutt	D	do	
Nelson M Welch	D	do	
Cyrus M Baker	D	do	
William Fogg	E	do	
John Bradley	E	do	
Frank Bean	E	do	
Johnson Bachelder	E	do	
Isaac Chapman	E	do	
John F Stone	E	do	
William Wentworth	E	do	
James L Hill	E	do	
David H Abbott	E	do	
Simeon P Ayer	E	do	
Joshua Brown	E	do	
Thomas G Binford	E	do	
Israel Day jr	E	do	
Hiram Frost	E	do	
John P Fenderson	E	do	
Fredk W Knight	E	do	
Frank Plummer	E	do	
Ira Ramsell jr	E	do	
Fernando C Tarr	E	do	
Geo W Warren	E	do	
Byron Ford	F	do	
Joseph L Brown	F	do	
Jarvis C Cooper	F	do	
John Q A Vining	F	do	
Isaac Bonney	F	do	
Freeman J Emery	F	do	
Ariel R Prescott	G	do	
Winslow J Gordon	G	do	
Wm H Bither	G	do	
James N Crane	G	do	
Geo B Fisher	G	do	
Adolphus E Harlow	G	do	
Geo W Lord	G	do	
John Mangan	G	do	
Joseph Neely	G	do	
Sidney H Sinclair	G	do	
Hugh Monroe	G	do	
Daniel Anderson	G	do	
Martin V Guptill	G	do	
Benj F Lord	G	do	
Wm Miller	G	do	
James Pelton	G	do	
Albert S Palmer	G	do	
Edgar F Page	G	do	
James Smith	G	do	
Henry Weymouth	G	do	
Marshal N Colcord	H	do	

NINTH REGIMENT INFANTRY, (Continued.)

Discharged.—Time Expired.

Names.	Co.	Date.	Remarks.
Geo T Cunningham	H	Sept. 27, 1861.	
Wm A Killon	H	do	
Joseph Weeks	H	do	
Lewis F Yeaton	H	do	
Moses Haley	H	do	
Chas M Johnson	H	do	
Wm A Lombard	H	do	
Llewellyn D Smith	H	do	
Henry B Chatterly	I	do	
Stephen Colson	I	do	
Geo W Califf	I	do	
James Davis	I	do	
Wm S Frazier	I	do	
Otis J Giles	I	do	
Warren E Jordan	I	do	
Chas S Stone	I	do	
James W Town	I	do	
Rufus B Sprague	I	do	
John F Burton	I	do	
Geo W Furbush	I	do	
Chas L Jepson	I	do	
Dennis Mahoney	I	do	
Geo W Richardson	I	do	
John F Stevens	I	do	
Wm P Sturgis	K	do	
Geo W Johnson	K	do	
James F Smith	R	do	
Van B Bray	K	do	
Geo B Gustin	K	do	
Benj F Goodwin	K	do	
Forrest R Higgins	K	do	
Frank B Libby	K	do	
Wm H H Merrill	K	do	
Moses Austin	K	do	
Andrew J Avery	K	do	
Hiram Gustin	K	do	
Robert N Morrill	K	do	
James N Nickerson	K	do	
Wm H Sturgis	K	do	

Deceased.

T B Brown	D	Aug. 12, 1861.	From wounds received in action.
R Rowe	D	Sept. 17,	Of disease.
Ira Cole	E	Aug. 21,	do
Augustus McCauley	E	" 5,	From wounds received in action.
Clark Millett	F	" 14,	Of disease.
John A Forsyth	G	" 13,	From wounds received in action.
Solomon J Watson	D	Sept. 29,	Killed in action.
Llewellyn Frederick	D	" 29,	do
Greenlief Parker	E	" 29,	do
Joseph D Norcross	I	" 8,	From wounds received in action.

Missing.

John Hall	A	Sept. 29, 1861.	In action at Chapin's Farm, Va.
Oscar M Whiting	C	" 29,	do
Nelson Towle	E	" 29,	do

NINTH REGIMENT INFANTRY, (Continued.)

Missing.

Names.	Co.	Date.	Remarks.
Chas W Morrill	E	Sept. 29, 1864.	In action at Chapin's Farm, Va.
C E Eastman	E	" 29,	do
Ezra M Perry	F	" 29,	do
Bertram Dillingham	G	" 29,	do
Hiram Twist	G	" 29,	do
Jacob C Lane	G	" 29,	do
James A Bates	H	" 29,	do
John N Given	H	" 29,	do
John W Foss	H	" 29,	do
Thomas Kent	I	" 29,	do
E Hart	K	" 29,	do

October, 1864.

Returned from Desertion.

John E Cushing	G	May 1, 1864.	Omitted in previous return.

Deserted.

Edward B Sanderson	P.Mus.	Aug. 11, 1864.	From hospital.
John Coy	A	Oct. 15,	At Chapin's Farm, Va.
William Burns	A	" 15,	do
John Donahue	A	" 21,	do do to the enemy.
James Devereaux	A	" 21,	do do do
G H Brown	B	Sept. 23,	At Augusta, Me.
Joseph P Littlefield	C	Aug. 28,	From hospital.
Henry Knowles	B	Oct. 5,	At Chapin's Farm, Va.

Discharged.

Alonzo J Moody	B	Oct. 22, 1864.	Time expired.
Wm O Blackman	B	Sept. 22,	do

Deceased.

Jason M Prescott	D	Oct. 27, 1864.	Killed in action.
Moses H Judkins	I	Sept. 18,	From wounds received in action.
Thomas Linnare	I	Oct. 20,	do
F E Baker	K	" 27,	Killed in action.
R Downs	K	" 27,	do

Returned from Missing in Action.

Jerry Foley	G	Oct. 31, 1864.	At Chapin's Farm, Va.
Robert F Emerson	H	" 31,	do

TENTH REGIMENT INFANTRY, (2 years.)

Mustered into U. S. service Oct. 4, 1861, to serve two years from May 3d, 1861, and mustered out May 8th, 1864, at Portland, Me., by Capt. Thos. C. J. Baily, 17th U. S. Infantry.

Cos. A and D, together with the recruits of this regiment, mustered in for three years, were organized into a Battalion of three companies, and known as Battalion Tenth Regiment Infantry, lettered companies A, B and D.

BATTALION TENTH REGIMENT INFANTRY.

Transferred to 29th Regt. Infantry, Vet. Vols.

ELEVENTH REGIMENT INFANTRY.

August, 1864.

Returned from Desertion.

Names.	Co.	Date.	Remarks.
W H Johnson	A	Aug. 22, 1864.	At Deep Bottom, Va.

Returned from Transferred.

Names.	Co.	Date.	Remarks.
Hiram W Woodman	D	Aug. 2, 1864.	From V. R. Corps.
James H Taylor	G	" 29,	do

Deceased.

Names.	Co.	Date.	Remarks.
Moses Gross	A	Aug. 11, 1864.	Killed in action.
James McGinnis	C	" 11,	do
Charles E Urann	C	" 11,	do
S S Beadle	C	" 14,	do
John N Stanley	D	" 11,	do
Harvey C Shephard	D	" 11,	do
John W Hall	D	" 11,	do
Andrew McCleavo	F	" 11,	do
Amos W Briggs	G	" 11,	do
G A Buckman	A	" 16,	do
Chas J Jordan	A	" 16,	do
J L Mitchell	A	" 16,	do
J L Potter	B	" 16,	do
J T French	B	" 16,	do
E G Hanscomb	D	" 16,	do
W A Quimby	E	" 16,	do
Aug E Hall	F	" 16,	do
G F Morrell	H	" 16,	do
L R Smith	H	" 16,	do
Randolph A Shorey	I	" 16,	do
James Andrews	A	July 30,	From wounds received in action.
Daniel A Bean	A	June 6,	do
Daniel O Butler	A	" 15,	do
Thomas D Cook	A	July 4,	do
James N Leighton	C	Aug. 4,	do
Horace H Bearco	E	July 28,	do
Enoch E Hinkley	F	Aug. 16,	do
A V Vandine	I	July 11,	do
Stephen Thurston	K	" 27,	do
J W Tibbetts	A	" 9,	Of disease.
G W Swett	C	Aug. 16,	do
T A Crosby	D	" 27,	do
George Allen	D	" 15,	do
J D S True	G	June 7,	do
W D Trask	G	July 11,	do

Missing.

Names.	Co.	Date.	Remarks.
Geo C Gould	K	Aug. 1, 1864.	In action at Deep Bottom, Va

Transferred.

Names.	Co.	Date.	Remarks.
Daniel McFell	I	Aug. 1, 1864.	To V. R. Corps.

ELEVENTH REGIMENT INFANTRY, (Continued.)
SEPTEMBER, 1864.
Returned from Desertion.

Names.	Co	Date.	Remarks.
Chas C Speed	E		Erroneously reported a deserter.

Deceased.

Names.	Co	Date.	Remarks.
Thomas D Tainter	A	Sept. 12, 1864.	From wounds received in action.
M Doyle	A	" 14,	do
Henry L Blake	B	" 4,	do
Lewis H Wing	F	" 11,	Killed in action.
Daniel B Snow	I	Aug. 19,	From wounds received in action.
James W Moody	I	" 18,	do
Asa A Arthurs	I	Sept. 19,	Killed in his tent by sharpshooter.
David Peabody	K	Aug. 16,	From wounds received in action.
Irwin L Prentiss	K	Sept. 14,	do
Abner F Bassett	D	" 15,	Killed in action.
S A Bragdon	D	Aug. 15,	From wounds received in action.
Adelbert P Stratton	D	" 15,	do
Jas W Wilkinson	A	Sept. 2,	Of disease.
Reuben H Small	A	" 16,	do
Erastus O Whitney	B	Aug. 25,	do
George P Reed	C	Sept. 13,	do
Eugene Bragdon	E		do at Fort Monroe.
Cyrus Handy	G	Aug. 28, 1864.	Of disease.
George McGlinch	G	" 28,	do
John W Kenney	I	" 19,	do
Chas W Lawrence	K	" 5,	do

Transferred.

Names.	Co	Date.	Remarks.
Chas C Speed	E		To V. R. Corps.

OCTOBER, 1864.
Deserted.

Names.	Co	Date.	Remarks.
Morton Moody	I	Oct. 6, 1864.	While on furlough.

Deceased.

Names.	Co	Date.	Remarks.
Reuben H Cross	H	Oct. 7, 1864.	Killed in action.
Joseph Meader	H	" 7,	do
Melville G Nye	B	" 13,	do
Erastus J Mansur	A	" 13,	From wounds received in action.
Aaron Gomery	A	Sept. 18,	do
Horace W Brown	A	June 2,	do
Rodney C Harriman	F	Sept. 26,	do
Ira D Toothaker	F	" 21,	do
Ezra Smith	C	" 14,	do
Wm P Weymouth	D	Sept. 2,	do
Wm Sherman	D	" 1,	do
Frank Bubier	D	" 13,	do
Archibald Taggard	G	Oct. 3,	do
Geo H Woodward	A	Sept. 17,	Of disease.
Henry D Otis	G	" 17,	do
George Goor	I	Oct. 22,	do
John Milton	I	" 11,	do
Elias A Briggs	H	Sept. 25,	do

Transferred.

Names.	Co	Date.	Remarks.
James Rutherford	F		To V. R. Corps.
Luther E Maddocks	K		do

ELEVENTH REGIMENT INFANTRY, (Continued.)

On account of the delay which must necessarily occur in the publication of the next return, it was thought proper to publish in this return a list of the enlisted men of the detachment of the Eleventh Regiment Infantry mustered out at Augusta, Maine, (time having expired,) rather than delay it for the November return.

Names.	Co.	Date.	Remarks.
Elias P Morton	S. Maj.	Nov. 18, 1864.	
William Wiley	C. Sgt.	do	
Abner Brooks	Pr Mus	do	
Joseph Webb	A	do	
James R Stone	A	do	
William G Lee	A	do	
James H Giles	A	do	
Frank E Noyes	A	do	
Sylvester Stone	A	do	
Francis M Burton	A	do	
Benj R Bibber	A	do	
John Ballard	A	do	
George Lynch	A	do	
Phineas Witham	A	do	
Charles W Bridgham	C	do	
Edwin I Miller	C	do	
James Gross	C	do	
Allen M Cole	C	do	
Asa W Googings	C	do	
William Libby	C	do	
Melville Cole	C	do	
Frederick W Cannon	C	do	
Asa K Smith	C	do	
Charles Skinner	C	do	
Wm F Elwell	C	do	
Elijah S Kelley	C	do	
Harrison Hayford	C	do	
George W Saunders	C	do	
Ephraim Francis	D	do	
John Dyer	D	do	
Amaziah Hunter	D	do	
Wm H Darling	D	do	
Matthew P House	D	do	
Hiram A Woolman	D	do	
Moses Carver	D	do	
Melvin Conforth	D	do	
Moniram J Fisher	E	do	
Ira Weymouth	E	do	
Franklin C Rowe	E	do	
Andrew R Patten	E	do	
L Lassell	E	do	
Kenney C Lowell	E	do	
William Clark jr	E	do	
J H Chadbourne	E	do	
Daniel S Cole	E	do	
Joseph H Ferguson	E	do	
Daniel W King	E	do	
Michael Lyons	E	do	
Ira F Gross	E	do	
Chas K Glidden	E	do	
Chas A Mansell	E	do	
David Simpson	E	do	
Daniel S Smith	F	do	

7

ELEVENTH REGIMENT INFANTRY, (Continued.)

Enlisted men mustered out, etc.

Names.	Co.	Date.	Remarks.
James W Bailey	F	Nov. 18, 1864.	
James W Little	F	do	
Rufus N Burgess	F	do	
Ambrose F Walsh	F	do	
George E Stickney	F	do	
Daniel Austin	F	do	
William Denene	F	do	
Franklin N Hayden	F	do	
Wendell F Joy	F	do	
Thomas C Jones	F	do	
Herman Kelley	F	do	
John E Morrill	F	do	
Darius Moulton	F	do	
Ira M Rollins	F	do	
Randall S Webb	F	do	
George S Buker	F	do	
Thomas C Blaisdell	F	do	
Harmon J Dill	F	do	
David G Graffam	F	do	
Albert Flye	G	do	
Charles A Lincoln	G	do	
Ambrose P Phillips	G	do	
Joshua Cunningham	G	do	
James H Taylor	G	do	
Asa B Young	G	do	
George W Cook	G	do	
Wm H Girrill	H	do	
James Ellis	H	do	
Augustus T Thompson	H	do	
John S Fogg	H	do	
John E Gould	H	do	
James Bachelder	H	do	
Francis S Gower	H	do	
Josiah Locke	H	do	
Nathaniel Moody	H	do	
Eben G Prescott	H	do	
Nathan J Gould	H	do	
Joseph Harris	H	do	
John Lary jr	H	do	
Edward L Ball	H	do	
James E Dunphey	H	do	
L J Livermore	H	do	
Geo P Moody	H	do	
Frank K Freeborn	H	do	
Joseph S Butler	I	do	
Chas W Trott	I	do	
Loren Garcy	I	do	
Justus S Huff	I	do	
Geo W Kinnee	I	do	
George Leader	I	do	
Daniel Morrissey	I	do	
Samuel G Braman	I	do	
Madison M Golding	I	do	
Thomas Kelley	I	do	
John Knox 1st	I	do	
Rufus K Shorey	I	do	
Geo W Young	I	do	

ELEVENTH REGIMENT INFANTRY, (Continued.)

Enlisted men mustered out, etc.

Names.	Co.	Date.	Remarks.
Henry H Davis	K	Nov. 18, 1864.	
John Howard	K	do	
Andrew B Erskine	K	do	
Charles Knowles	K	do	
Jotham S Garnett	K	do	
W Davis	K	do	
Roger A Erskine	K	do	
John Green	K	do	
Henry I Moore	K	do	
George Warrick	K	do	
Warren L Whittier	K	do	
Josiah Furbish	K	do	
Calvin S Chapman	K	do	
Charles E Morton	K	do	
Robert Ricker	K	do	
Samuel V Wentworth	K	do	

N. B. The Eleventh Regiment has been re-organized and is still in the field.

TWELFTH REGIMENT INFANTRY.

August, 1864.

Deserted.

Jacob Coffin	C	July 23, 1864.	At Bermuda Hundreds, Va.
Francis Hamel	D	" 13,	At Algiers, La.
John McDonald	D	" 13,	do
Charles E Edmonds	G	June 1,	At Portland, Me.
Adolphus Fritag	I	July 20,	At New Orleans, La.

Returned from Desertion.

Moses Merrill	K	Aug. 20, 1864.	At Halltown, Va.

Discharged.

M C Bacon	E	Aug. 16, 1864.	For insanity.
Stephen G Monson	E	July 16,	For disability.
David B Chesley	F	Aug. 8,	For promotion.
J Fortier	F	July 16,	
Joseph W Thompson	I	Aug. 13,	For promotion.

Deceased.

Charles Plummer	B	July 11, 1864.	At New Orleans, La.

September, 1864.

No returns received.

October, 1864.

Deserted.

John R Coolbroth	C	Sept. 19, 1864.	At Winchester, Va.
G Bragdon	H	" 19,	do
G W Smith	H	" 19,	do

Returned from Desertion.

I Rodriques	D	Oct. 12, 1864.	To take effect March 13, 1864.

TWELFTH REGIMENT INFANTRY, (Continued.)

Discharged.

Names.	Co.	Date.	Remarks.
O B Churchill	G	Oct. 12, 1864.	For disability.

Deceased.

Names.	Co.	Date.	Remarks.
Thomas Darrell	B	Sept. 24, 1864.	Of disease.
A Prue	C	Aug. 11,	do
Thomas Wood	C	" 23,	do
H F Farr	C	Oct. 19,	do
S Carter	D	" 7,	do
Alvah B Phelps	E	" 19,	Killed in action.
Eugene B Stinson	F	" —,	From wounds received in action.
J Adams	F	" 19,	Killed in action.
Chas D Garnett	F	" 19,	do
Cyrus L Seavey	F	" 19,	do
Franklin Tibbetts	F	" 19,	do
W H Harvey	F	Aug. 20,	On boat transport.
James G Cushing	K	Oct. 19,	Killed in action.

The time of service of the Twelfth Regiment Infantry having expired, the original members entitled to be discharged were ordered to Portland and were there mustered out.

The re-enlisted men and recruits were organized into a Battalion of four companies under Lt. Col. Illsley, and will hereafter be designated the 1st Battalion, 12th Regiment Infantry.

A list of the enlisted men of the 12th Regiment Infantry mustered out at Portland, is herein published. It should have been published in the December return, but on account of the delay which must occur before its publication, it was thought proper to insert such list in this return.

List of enlisted men of 12th Maine Volunteers mustered out at Portland.

Franklin Martin	A	Dec. 7, 1864.
Elbridge G Grover	A	do
Wm K Moore	A	do
Elisha M Boobier	A	do
Henry M Carpenter	A	do
Newell Cook	A	do
Geo F McDonald	A	do
Charles D Rowe	A	do
Jonathan V Silver	A	do
Charles H Blake	B	do
Leander Holmes	B	do
John Griffin	B	do
Ransom B Crook	B	do
George E Coffin	B	do
Simon Dearborn	B	do
Francis Keenan	B	do
Chas H Leighton	B	do
George W Luke	B	do
B M Lombard	B	do
John R Merrill	B	do
Andrew Perry	B	do
George Strout	B	do
John W Whitehead	B	do
James S Wood	B	do
Charles E Welch	B	do
Daniel P York	B	do
John S Abbott	C	do

TWELFTH REGIMENT INFANTRY. (Continued.)

Enlisted men mustered out, etc.

Names.	Co.	Date.	Remarks.
Thomas C Pratt	C	Dec. 7, 1864.	
Jefferson W Libbey	C	do	
George W Pillsbury	C	do	
Seth T Winslow	C	do	
Simon M Moses	C	do	
Wm C Allen	C	do	
Elias B Berry	C	do	
Marshall Emery	C	do	
George H Fogg	C	do	
Thomas J Libby	C	do	
Mervil S Merrill	C	do	
Theodore A Royal	C	do	
Bartlett F Waterhouse	C	do	
Augustus J Hall	D	do	
Charles A Wait	D	do	
Manville Wait	D	do	
Irving B Parker	D	do	
John Andrews	D	do	
Charles R Bartlett	D	do	
George W Berry	D	do	
Henry W Carville	D	do	
John H Doble	D	do	
George F Drown	D	do	
Chas H Kidder	D	do	
Orrison R Newton	D	do	
Elmore S Phelps	D	do	
Seymore A Farrington	D	do	
Samuel Knight	D	do	
Henry M Stearns	D	do	
Osgood H Watson	D	do	
Abel Ingalls	D	do	
John Fox	E	do	
Cornelius S Mace	E	do	
James C Stearns	E	do	
Timothy Stearns	E	do	
Thaxter B Safford	E	do	
Gilman Wallace	E	do	
Levi W Edgerly	F	do	
Albert Conn	F	do	
John A Dicker	F	do	
Joseph Gary	F	do	
Howdy H Adams	F	do	
Oscar Butters	F	do	
J K Champion	F	do	
Gabriel A Foster	F	do	
Luther M Hill	F	do	
Wm O Henderson	F	do	
Aaron Hinson	F	do	
Edwin Hanson	F	do	
Moses Lagers	F	do	
Edward S Page	F	do	
James St Coolidge	F	do	
Leonard H Titcomb	F	do	
Benj F Walker	F	do	
Wm H Lovejoy	G	do	
John W Lombard	G	do	
Geo L Watson	G	do	

TWELFTH REGIMENT INFANTRY, (Continued.)

Enlisted men mustered out, etc.

Names.	Co.	Date.	Remarks.
James S Davie	G	Dec. 7, 1864.	
Isaac F Durrell	G	do	
Henry H Dudley	G	do	
H W Grover	G	do	
James R Holt	G	do	
Emerson Kimball	G	do	
John H Lovejoy	G	do	
Randall F Mayberry	G	do	
Lewis Mitchell	G	do	
John Stevens	G	do	
Simon G Smith	G	do	
Calvin Soper	G	do	
Wm W Watson	G	do	
Laforest Voter	G	do	
Lewis H Watson	H	do	
Eugene Kingman	H	do	
Lewis H Bradbury	H	do	
Geo P Underwood	H	do	
Geo F Burton	H	do	
Samuel W Cole	H	do	
George Goff	H	do	
Wm K Harvey	H	do	
Wm B McKenney	H	do	
Josiah P Nickerson	H	do	
Jeremiah O'Neal	H	do	
Henry A Reed	H	do	
A B Towle	H	do	
Edwin Tuttle	H	do	
Henry Tyler	H	do	
John M Blanchard	I	do	
Wm Labenstein	I	do	
John W Torsey	I	do	
William Smith	K	do	
Freeman R Earle	K	do	
Wm H Earle	K	do	
A B Bridges	K	do	
Rufus G Chapman	K	do	
James E Goff	K	do	
Peter Lane	K	do	
Thomas McGuire	K	do	
Hugh McInnis	K	do	
John McClure	K	do	
Joseph H Neely	K	do	
Arthur Rice	K	do	
Chas W Sherman	K	do	
James H Smith	K	do	
Jeremiah Sterritt	K	do	

THIRTEENTH REGIMENT INFANTRY.

AUGUST, 1864.

Deserted.

Names.	Co	Date.	Remarks.
Bowman Wood	B	July 6, 1864.	At New Orleans, La.
John Gatewood	B	" 6,	do
Daniel Mahoney	B	" 6,	do
Frank Stearns	B	" 6,	do
M West	E	" 4,	do
N Green	F	" 1,	do
G H Fox	I	" 5,	do
John Morrison	I	" 5,	do
Wm G Roberts	I	" 5,	do

Returned from Desertion.

Wm H Phelps	H	Aug. 11, 1864.	At Augusta, Me.

Discharged.

Albion Adams	E		At New Orleans, La
Geo M Myrick	C		For disability.

Deceased.

Henry C Chase	B	July —, 1864.	From wounds received in action.
Martin W Pease	C	Jan. 14,	At Brownville, Texas.
Chas O Litchfield	C	July 6,	Of disease.
Thomas Adams	C	" 31,	do
Andrew Byler jr	C	Aug. 26,	do
Plummer M Farmer	E		Drowned.
James H Peavy	E	Aug. 17,	At Phillips, Me.
Joseph L Sawyer	E		Of disease.
Joseph D Wyman	E		At Washington, D. C.
E R Littlehale	H	Aug. 31,	Of disease.
L B Twitchell	H	" 20,	do
Everett Leighton	I	July 9,	do

Transferred.

William T Overlock	A	July 2, 1864.	To V. R. Corps.
E D Pinkham	A	" 2,	do
Benjamin Priest	B		To Invalid Corps.
Joseph Foss	C		do

SEPTEMBER, 1864.

Deserted.

Sewall Brassbridge	A	July 5, 1864.	At New Orleans, La.
Alfred Buswell	A	Sept. 21,	At Augusta, Me., while on furlough
Charles Herrick	A	" 21,	do
John Arno	A	July 5,	At New Orleans, La.
Benjamin Blow	A	" 5,	do
James Harrod	A	" 6,	do
Thomas Meigs	A	" 6,	do
Wesley Carville	C	Sept. 18,	At Augusta, Me., while on furlough.
Nelson V Graham	E	" 18,	do
Thomas Kenney	G	" 23,	do
T W Colbroth	G	" 2,	do
S V Young	G	" 26,	do
Charles A Coffin	H	" 26,	do
Granville W Drew	H	" 26,	do

THIRTEENTH REGIMENT INFANTRY, (Continued.)

Deserted.

Names.	Co.	Date.	Remarks.
Fred A Beattie	H	Sept. 26, 1864.	At Augusta, Me., while on furlough.
Matthew Hood	I	" 27,	do
Moses Leighton	I	" 27,	do
Alden Robinson	I	" 27,	do
John Ramsdell	I	" 27,	do
Tyler Robinson	I	" 27,	do
John L O'Mara	I	" 27,	do
Joseph A Shea	I	" 27,	do
Harris Whitten	I	" 27,	do
Geo F Eldridge	I	" 27,	do
J F Fellows	K	" 26,	do

Discharged.

Lyman D King	I		At New Orleans, La.
Wm H Cates	I		do
Erastus C Wheeler	P.Mus.	July 3, 1864.	For disability.

Deceased.

Orlando Mansfield	G	April 13, 1864.	From wounds received in action.

Transferred.

Elisha T Preble	H	Sept. 24, 1864.	To invalid corps.

Returned from Missing in Action.

John Reed	G	Sept. 22, 1864.	At Augusta, Me.

OCTOBER, 1864.

Deserted.

James N Dunn	A	Sept. 28, 1864.	At New York.
Thaddeus Green	C	" 27,	At Augusta, Me.
W W Campbell	D	Oct. 12,	do
George Davis	H	" 1,	At Boston, Mass.

Discharged.

A Chase	B	Sept. 24, 1864.	For disability.
Geo B Mason	B	June 20,	do
W J Coolbroth	C		do

Deceased.

Wm R Grout	A	June 7, 1864.	At New Orleans, La.
Eben Eldridge	G		do
Isaac D White	G		On passage from Texas.
Addison H Beach	K	July 24, 1864.	At New Orleans, La.
J Nesbitt	K	Aug. 4,	do
Isaac Johnston	K	Oct. 12,	At Martinsburg, Va.
W D W Walker	H	" 14,	Accidentally.

FOURTEENTH REGIMENT INFANTRY.

August, 1864.

Deserted.

Names.	Co.	Date.	Remarks.
Michael Chisham	D	July 24, 1864.	At Bermuda Hundreds, Va.
John P Greely	F	" 29,	At Deep Bottom, Va.
Frank Webber	G	May 21,	At New Orleans, La.

Returned from Desertion.

Christopher Spangler	C	Aug. 14, 1864.	At Tennallytown, D. C.

Discharged.

Amos H Allen	A	Feb. 18, 1864.	For disability.
Christian Packard	I	July 6,	do

Transferred.

Thomas Bennett	A	May 31, 1864.	To V. R. Corps.
Seth S Colby	A	June 30,	To U. S. navy.
Edward Nabis	A	" 30,	do
Elwin Ordway	A	" 30,	do
Joseph H Staples	A	" 30,	do
Joseph C Ware	A	" 30,	do
Arthur Bridges	A	" 30,	do
Wm F Osgood	A	" 30,	do
Henry Richardson	A	" 30,	do
Irving Morse	A	" 30,	do
Emory Worthly	C	" 30,	do
Wm P Turner	C	" 30.	do
Alex Adams	C	" 30,	do
John Braislin	C	" 30,	do
Andrew Downs	C	May 31,	To V. R. Corps.
John H Roche	E	" 30,	do
Wm L Hines	G	" 31,	do

Dropped from the Rolls.

Henri Poggenpohl	G		Never heard fm since sent to hosp. Aug. 1st

SEPTEMBER, 1864.

Returned from Desertion.

Elliott P Witham	K	Sept. 16, 1864.	At Berryville, Va.

Discharged.

George Silley	K	Aug. 10, 1864.	For disability.

Deceased.

Charles Baldic	C	Sept. 19, 1864.	Killed in action.
James McGinnis	C		Of disease, at New Orleans, La.
D Thompson	E	Sept. 19, 1864.	Killed in action.
Chas F Staples	E	" 19,	do
James P Harris	G	" 19,	do
Ludwig Ehlert	G	" 19,	do
George Miller	H	" 19,	do

OCTOBER, 1864.

Deceased.

A L Belan	D	Oct. 19, 1864.	Killed in action.
D D Costigan	F	" 19,	do
W N Dill	F	May 29,	Of disease.
John Kochler	G	Oct. 19,	Killed in action.
Henry Myers	H	" 19,	do
F O Dudley	H	Sept. 3,	Of disease.

8

(58)

FIFTEENTH REGIMENT INFANTRY.

August, 1864.

Deserted.

Names.	Co.	Date.	Remarks.
J A Finnerty	K	July 5, 1864.	At New Orleans, La.

Deceased.

Richard Ryan	A	Aug. 3, 1864.	From wounds received in action.
William E Campbell	A	" 3,	Of disease.
James Bell	C		do
Samuel Miller	F	July 15,	do

Transferred.

Amos P Archibald	D	April 30, 1864.	To V. R. Corps.

September, 1864.

Deceased.

James Coombs	B		Of disease, at Baton Rouge, La.
Simeon Gage	B		do at Harper's Ferry, Va.
Samuel Miller	F	July 15, 1864.	do at N. Orleans, La.
Miles W Averill	G		do do
Samuel Fitzherbert	G		do do
George Marks	G		do at Washington, D. C.

October, 1864.

Deserted.

Duncan Faulkner	D	Sept. 17, 1864.	At Augusta, Me., while on furlough.
Alexander Noble	D	do	do
Sidney Verrill	D	do	do
George R Ray	D	do	do
P R Winslow	D	do	do
William Mitchell	F	do	do
William Ryan	F	do	do
Michael Higney	F	do	do
Frank Martin	F	do	do
James Maladay	F	do	do
Morris Murphy	F	do	do
John Mehegan	F	do	do
Joseph Cyr	G	do	do
Charles K Bolster	G	do	do
Maguire Dubay	G	do	do
William Duke	G	do	do
Thomas Dunnell	G	do	do
Francis Goven	G	do	do
William Morin	G	do	do
Fabian Crock	G	do	do
Raymond Cormier	G	do	do
Warren Robbins	H	do	do
Oscar A Coombs	H	do	do
James Burnham	I	July 5, 1864.	At New Orleans, La.
John A Finnerty	K	" 5,	do

Returned from Desertion.

James A Chamberlain	H	Oct. 2, 1864.	At Augusta, Me.
James Murphy	F	" 2,	do

FIFTEENTH REGIMENT INFANTRY, (Continued.)

Discharged.

Names.	Co.	Date.	Remarks.
Warren Fifield	E	Oct. 5, 1864.	For disability.
Chas R Mitchell	F	Sept. 21,	do

Deceased.

Peter Decoster	A	Sept. 17, 1864.	Of disease.
John E Thorndike	A	June 23,	do
Alfred F Perkins	E	Sept. 6,	do
Christopher Ballard	H	Aug. 10,	do
Ira P Hill	H	" 15,	do

Transferred.

George B Webber	E		To V. R. Corps.
Henry Hodgdon	G	Jan. 17, 1864.	do
Obadiah F Irish	G		do

SIXTEENTH REGIMENT INFANTRY.

August, 1864.

Returned from Desertion.

Jas A Stevens	A	Aug. 27, 1864.
Daniel G Putnam	D	" 27,
William Bolson	D	" 27,

Discharged.

Sumner W Turner	B	July 15, 1864. At Washington, D. C.
Edward A Locke	F	Dec. 24, 1863. do

Deceased.

Edwin C Stevens	S. Maj.	Aug. 18, 1864. Killed in action.
Amasa Cobb	E	July 25, Of disease.

Missing.

James Parsons	A	Aug. 19, 1864. In action at Weldon Railroad.
C C Williams	A	" 19, do
T T Whitcomb	A	" 19, do
Freeman T Knowles	A	" 19, do
S A Chamberlain	A	" 19, do
Freeman Brackett	A	" 19, do
Hugh Conway	A	" 19, do
James Fahey	A	" 19, do
A J Murch	A	" 18, do
Wm A Knowles	A	" 18, do
Timothy Ford	A	" 18, do
Benjamin Carville	A	" 18, do
Simeon Tripp	A	" 18, do
Henry Maddocks	B	" 19, do
Henry Mansfield	B	" 19, do
Clinton A Davis	B	" 19, do
Charles D Smith	B	" 19, do
A B Thayer	B	" 19, do
Allen Turner	B	" 19, do
Wm Farnum	C	" 19, do
Henry D Fisk	C	" 19, do

SIXTEENTH REGIMENT INFANTRY, (Continued.)

Missing.

Names.	Co.	Date.	Remarks.
Edward C Jones	C	Aug. 19, 1864.	In action at Weldon Railroad.
Madison J Grindle	C	" 19,	do
John O Allen	C	" 19,	do
John Anderson	C	" 19,	do
Martin Butterfield	C	" 19,	do
Hezekiel L Cole	C	" 19,	do
George W Evans	C	" 19,	do
Wm D Grant	C	" 19,	do
Charles H Gilman	C	" 19,	do
David H Hinds	C	" 19,	do
Elias Humphrey	C	" 19,	do
Archibald Phinney	C	" 19,	do
Henry A Thorp	C	" 19,	do
A W Spooney	C	" 19,	do
Silas H Scudder	C	" 19,	do
Chas W Wright	C	" 19,	do
Wm Farrar	C	" 19,	do
Charles Couture	C	" 19,	do
Timothy Butters	C	" 19,	do
Austin W Hobart	D	" 19,	do
S S Robertson	D	" 19,	do
Ezra S Seavey	D	" 19,	do
Joseph G Lamb	E	" 19,	do
Warren Simmond	E	" 18,	do
C F Blaisdell	E	" 19,	do
H F Judkins	E	" 19,	do
Stephen Buswell	E	" 19,	do
John Hartwell	E	" 19,	do
M Towle	E	" 19,	do
Charles W Ross	F	" 19,	do
Charles Goodrich	F	" 19,	do
Frank Leavitt	F	" 19,	do
Theodore Bussell	F	" 19,	do
W W Dunton	F	" 19,	do
Samuel Pierce	F	" 19,	do
Albert Powers	F	" 18,	do
John W Chadbourn	F	" 18,	do
Dennis Haley	F	" 18,	do
Geo W Smith	F	" 18,	do
John W Webster	F	" 18,	do
S T Farnham	G	" 19,	do
J H Train	G	" 19,	do
T Coleman	G	" 19,	do
Michael Doyle	G	" 19,	do
B Boyle	G	" 19,	do
P Leary	G	" 19,	do
L M Porter	G	" 19,	do
R S Morgan	G	" 19,	do
H J Read	G	" 19,	do
F S Sanders	G	" 19,	do
A Treat	G	" 19,	do
S H Chamberlain	G	" 19,	do
Geo W Fisher	H	" 18,	do
Wm Fennelly	H	" 18,	do
T D Witherly	H	" 18,	do
H A Chandler	H	" 18,	do
John Farley	H	" 18,	do

SIXTEENTH REGIMENT INFANTRY, (Continued.)

Missing.

Names.	Co.	Date.	Remarks.
Lewis Gilbert	H	Aug. 18, 1864.	In action at Weldon Railroad.
Jasper H Nash	H	" 18,	do
Chas R Atkins	H	" 18,	do
Charles Crampton	H	" 19,	do
Chas B Dore	H	" 19,	do
Lemuel T Hoyt	H	" 19,	do
Chas E Hatch	H	" 19,	do
Dennis Jenkins	H	" 19,	do
Thomas Middleton	H	" 19,	do
D Lovely	H	" 19,	do
Henry A Heal	H	" 19,	do
M L Whitten	H	" 19,	do
Geo B Haskell	I	" 19,	do
A H Briggs	I	" 19,	do
William Davis	I	" 19,	do
William Frazier	I	" 19,	do
Charles Thompson	I	" 19,	do
James Dutton	I	" 19,	do
George W Anderson	I	" 19,	do
Wesley Booker	I	" 19,	do
Jeremiah Banks	I	" 19,	do
Josiah Cornish	I	" 19,	do
Thomas Campbell	I	" 19,	do
Thomas Crosby	I	" 19,	do
Benjamin Colby	I	" 19,	do
James Dinning	I	" 19,	do
B F Garcelon	I	" 19,	do
S Holmes	I	" 19,	do
Oliver Stover	I	" 19,	do
C Mayo	K	" 18,	do
Eli C Lyons	K	" 18,	do
J B Marks	K	" 18,	do
Joseph Peacock	K	" 19,	do
Chas A Jordan	K	" 19,	do
Hezekiah Brown	K	" 19,	do
Alonzo Sanborn	K	" 19,	do
Calvin B Marks	K	" 19,	do

Returned from Missing in Action.

George A Field	G	Aug. 10, 1864.	

SEPTEMBER, 1864.

Deserted.

John Lyon	E	May 4, 1864.	At Mitchell's Station, Va.

Discharged.

Daniel W Marston	C	Sept. 20, 1864.	Time expired.
Jas W Richardson	B	" 15,	For disability.
Thomas J Gould	F	" 6,	do
Sidney A Allen	E		By civil authority.

Deceased.

Albert W Roberts	D	Aug. 7, 1864.	Of disease.

SIXTEENTH REGIMENT INFANTRY, (Continued.)

Transferred.

Names.	Co.	Date.	Remarks.
Edward P Snow	A	Sept. 1, 1864.	To V. R. Corps.
Leonard Gross	C	" 15,	do
John Heath	E		do

Returned from Missing in Action.

Albert C Holbrook	A	Sept. 7, 1864.	
E Low	B	" 7,	

OCTOBER, 1864.

The return for this month has been received, and shows enlisted men discharged 2, deceased 2, and deserted 3; but on account of the loss of part of the return, the names cannot be given before a list can be procured from the regiment, to appear in the next return.

SEVENTEENTH REGIMENT INFANTRY.

AUGUST, 1864.

Returned from Desertion.

Charles Smith	D	Aug. —, 1864.	
D B Ricker	F	" 27,	
J N Paine	I	" 26,	

Deserted.

R B Avery	A		
Francis H Barnes	A		
S D Roberts	A		
C H Howard	D	May 5, 1864.	
Martin Harrington	D		
H Milford	D		
M L Deering	F	Aug. 29, 1864.	
Cyrus H Hill	G	July 30,	
B F Welch	H	Aug. 9,	
W A Ward	I	Oct. 12, 1863.	

Discharged.

Patrick McGrath	A	Aug. 7, 1864.	For disability.
T P Mitchell	E	" 17,	do
W E Strout	I		At Augusta, Me.
E A Warren	K	Aug. 3,	For disability.

Deceased.

G W Joy	A	Aug. 18, 1864.	From wounds received in action.
Chas H Merrill	B	July 29,	do
Joseph McGrath	B		do
Charles Eastman	C	July 14,	do
G F Bliss	D	" 6,	Of disease.
Samuel McDonald	E	Aug. 3,	do
A S Curtis	G	" 20,	do
Leonard Pride	H	June 23,	do
John Roberts	I	Aug. 15,	do
J W Spruce	I	May 24,	do
Albion Kennison	K	Aug. 3,	do

SEVENTEENTH REGIMENT INFANTRY, (Continued.)

Transferred.

Names.	Co.	Date.	Remarks.
Charles Milliken	A	Aug. 5, 1864.	To V. R. Corps.
Edward Fabyan	A	" 5,	do
S H Waldron	B	" 6,	do
George Hanna	D	" 6,	do
W Trafton	D	" 6,	do
Luther Childs	G	" 5,	do
Michael Hawley	G	" 8,	do
T O Whitney	G	" 6,	do
Robert Benson	I	June 18,	do

Missing.

Names	Co.	Date	Remarks
William Bryne	A	Nov. 27, 1863.	In action.
A P Millett	A	May 12, 1864.	do
Daniel Cohan	A	" 12,	do
Charles Alexander	B		do
R G Curtis	B	May 6, 1864.	do
F W Chase	D	June 7,	do

Returned from Missing in Action.

S B Wing	K	Aug. 11, 1864.	

SEPTEMBER, 1864.

Deserted.

Charles O Perry	F	Sept. —, 1864.	From hospital.
John Fuller	G	" 1,	At Petersburg, Va.

Discharged.

Wm W Stone	A	Sept. 21, 1864.	Term expired.
H C Johnson	C	" 30,	do
E P Hannon	D	" 7,	By order general court martial.
John H Waterman	G	" 7,	At Portland, Me.

Deceased.

Frederick Cook	G	Sept. 21, 1864.	Killed in action.
Benj J Haley	H	" 7,	Of disease.
Caleb L Miller	I	" 17,	Killed on picket.
Eugene Stackpole	I	Aug. 21,	Of disease.

Transferred.

D S N Thurlow	C	Sept. 27, 1864.	To V. R. Corps.
Allen M Churchill	C	" 27,	do
John Hogan	D	" 27,	do
James M Blake	E	" 9,	do
Albert H Perry	G	" 12,	do
Joseph Hill	I		do

Returned from Missing in Action.

Henry F Hunt	A	Sept. 1, 1864	At Petersburg, Va.
William Herrin	C	" 2,	At Parole Camp.

OCTOBER, 1864.

Deserted.

Tobias Gould	C	June 1, 1864.	While on furlough.
Wm R Carl	H	Oct. 18,	do

SEVENTEENTH REGIMENT INFANTRY, (Continued.)

Discharged.

Names.	Co.	Date.	Remarks.
H H Shaw	A	Oct. 8, 1864.	By order.
C B Elliott	C	" 10,	do
H C Johnson	C	" 1,	Time expired.
Orrin A Kittredge	E	" 9,	By order.
Chas M Bachelder	E	" 9,	do
Chas H Smiley	E	" 14,	do
George R Fickett	F	" 15,	For disability.
Charles Sprague	H	Aug. 19,	do
Joseph S Bachelder	I	Oct. 20,	Time expired.
Amos H Wall	I	" 7,	do

Deceased.

Names.	Co.	Date.	Remarks.
William Castle	B	Oct. 21, 1864.	From wounds received in action.
Enoch B Mayberry	C	" 11,	Killed in action.
P Soper	C	" 11,	do
Nathan Clifford	C	" 5,	Of disease.
George W Foster	C	Sept. 5,	do
Edward L Smith	E	Oct. 7,	do
Samuel Huff jr	E	" 14,	do
John J O'Connell	E	" 17,	Killed on picket.
Thomas B Perkins	F	" 24,	Of disease.
Charles Stewart	G	" 12,	do
George Jennings	G	Sept. 30,	do
N B Abbott	H	Oct. 8,	From wounds received in action.
D W Haskell	H	" 7,	do
John Brown 2d	I	" 10,	Of disease.
Geo E Sherburn	K	" 17,	Killed on picket.
Joseph F Tufts	K	" 6,	Of disease.

Transferred.

Names.	Co.	Date.	Remarks.
George T Jones	A	Oct. 21, 1864.	To V. R. Corps.
W H Chick	A	" 21,	do
A A Ford	C	Aug. 22,	do
Charles H Patten	D	Oct. 20,	do
Edwin G Baker	D	" 20,	do
Patrick Kelly	H	Sept. 27,	do
Sylvanus B Estes	H	Oct. 20.	do

Missing.

Names.	Co.	Date.	Remarks.
John Lakin	F	Oct. 28, 1864.	In action.
George F Jellison	G	May 12,	do at Spottsylvania C. H.
Orrin Rogers	G	" 10,	do do

Returned from Missing in Action.

Names.	Co.	Date.
W L Faunce	C	Oct. 25, 1864.

EIGHTEENTH REGIMENT INFANTRY.

Mustered into the U. S. service August 21, 1862, for the term of three years. Was organized into the 1st Regiment Heavy Artillery, by order of the War Department, Dec. 19, 1862.

NINETEENTH REGIMENT INFANTRY.

August, 1864.

Returned from Desertion.

Names.	Co.	Date.	Remarks.
A Cunningham	C	Mar. 27, 1864.	

Deserted.

John Callaghan	A	July 30, 1864.	
J G Curtis	A	Aug. 20,	
F N Metcalf	B	May 4,	
J Lagerson	E	July 30,	From hospital.
R Johnson	F	Aug. 12,	
J Ballard	G	June 22,	

Discharged.

Robert Noble	A	July 19, 1864.	For disability.
W D Buckley	D	" 14,	do
H C Holmes	E	Aug. 7,	do
J Webster	A		For promotion.
J A Lord	D	Aug. 13, 1864.	do
G P Wood	G	July 19,	do
T P Beath	K	Aug. 10,	do
B P Dolloff	K	" 10,	do
T B Campbell	C	July 19,	do

Deceased.

O Lewis	A	July 28, 1864.	From wounds received in action.
J Rice	B	Aug. 1,	do
C A Chandler	B	July 2,	do
A N Clay	B	Aug. 26,	Killed in action.
A F Small	C	June 12,	From wounds received in action.
S H Johnson	D	July 22,	do
G F Doe	G	Aug. 25,	do
H Merrow	I	June 19,	do
H C Joyce	I	" 9,	Killed in action.

Missing in Action.

A V Gregory	B	Aug. 20, 1864.	At Reams' Station, Va.
A B Hall	B	" 20,	do
N Grover	B	" 20,	do
J W Barnes	C	" 20,	do
J H Flanders	C	" 20,	do
C Anderson	D	" 20,	do
W R Sawyer	D	" 20,	do
E Hollis	D	" 20,	do
N T Freeman	E	" 20,	do
E P Richards	E	" 20,	do
B Roberts	E	" 20,	do
T A Baker	F	" 20,	do
L B Ricker	F	" 20,	do
William Murphy	G	" 19,	At Deep Bottom, Va.
Y Young	G	" 25,	At Reams' Station, Va.
A J Bassford	H	" 25,	do
G L Smith	H	" 25,	do
C Steward	H	" 25,	do
C L Long	H	" 25,	do
L Boynton	I	" 25,	do
P Larkin	I	" 25,	do

NINETEENTH REGIMENT INFANTRY, (Continued.)

Missing in Action.

Names.	Co.	Date.	Remarks.
J D Madison	I	Aug. 25, 1864.	At Reams' Station, Va.
C Miles	I	" 25,	do
C Powell	I	" 25,	do
F York	I	" 25,	do
M Murry	K	" 25,	do
William Greenwood	K	" 25,	do
G H Bennett	K	" 25,	do

Transferred.

J Bachelder	B	Aug. 2, 1864.	From V. R. Corps.
Frank Brown	H	" 2,	do
A H Ellis	B	" 6,	To V. R. Corps.
L Dearborn	E	July 1,	do
R A Wentworth	F	Aug. —,	do
E H Hicks	G	" —,	To U. S. Navy.
C S Whitten	H	Mar. 31,	To V. R. Corps.
G M Perkins	H	" 15,	do
J G Maddocks	I	" 15,	do

SEPTEMBER, 1864.

Discharged.

A N Ulmer	B	Sept. 2, 1864.	Term expired.
H A Davis	C	" 19,	do
E Wade	C	" 7,	do
H Davis	G	" 8,	do
J M Eugley	H	" 6,	do
M Butler	I	" 30,	do
C H Williams	C	July 15,	For disability.
H Clapp	I	Sept. 15,	do
Silas Adams	F	" 3,	By order war department.
L W Holfses	D	Aug. 11,	For disability.

Deceased.

J Cilley	E	Aug. 30, 1864.	From wounds received in action.
C R Powers	G	July —,	do
A J Gray	C	" 27,	Of disease.

Transferred.

J A Tyler	E		To V. R. Corps.
W Hawes	K	Sept. 11, 1864.	do

Missing.

J O Bean	D	Aug. 25, 1864.	In action at Reams' Station, Va.
J W Young	D	" 25,	do
E B Curtis	K	" 25,	do

OCTOBER, 1864.

Deserted.

C F Spinney	K		While on furlough.
A Robinson	K		do
George Duval	Sergt.	Oct. 12, 1864.	From 5th Co. unas. inf. consolidated
J Bowman	Corp.	" 13,	do [with this regt.
C C Bennett	Priv.	" 13,	do
William Clough	"	" 13,	do

NINETEENTH REGIMENT INFANTRY, (Continued.)

Deserted.

Names.	Co.	Date.	Remarks.
William B Cook	Priv.	Oct. 13, 1864.	From 5th Co. unas. inf. consolidated
J Cummings	"	" 13,	do [with this regt.
J Davis	"	" 13,	do
J Duffy	"	" 13,	do
Wm F Floyd	"	" 13,	do
D McKelley	"	" 13,	do
J Kempt	"	" 13,	do
C Leonard	"	" 13,	do
Charles Lukius	"	" 13,	do
T Mangan	"	" 13,	do
V McNuttis	"	" 13,	do
J Montgomery	"	" 13,	do
J Nelson	"	" 13,	do
C Rice	"	" 13,	do
H Sweet	"	" 13,	do
J Martin	"	" 13,	do
E Thompson	"	" 13,	do
W Valentine	"	" 13,	do
P Wilson	"	" 13,	do
J Brown	"	" 13,	do

Discharged.

Names.	Co.	Date.	Remarks.
I J Rich	B	Oct. 5, 1864.	By order war department.
A B Plummer	F	" 6,	do
W H Tripp	H	" 29,	For promotion.
J Babson	I	" 29,	do
George Studley	I	" 29,	do

Deceased.

Names.	Co.	Date.	Remarks.
T M Heald	A	Oct. 27, 1864.	Killed in action.
A Hutchings	E	" 7,	do
George E Chase	F	" 22,	do
B Potter	G	" 5,	do
J Nelson	G	" 16,	do
J M Tyler	H	" 26,	do
George S Cobb	I	" 17,	do
William Metcalf	I		From wounds received in action.
D McMahon	H	Sept. 27,	Of disease.

Transferred.

Names.	Co.	Date.	Remarks.
D B Abbott	H	Aug. 10, 1864.	To V. R. Corps.

Missing.

Names.	Co.	Date.	Remarks.
D Bean	A	Oct. 27, 1864.	In action at Hatchee Run.
L Pinkham	F	" 27,	do
J A Wheeler	F	" 27,	do
M Lewis	G	" 28,	do
P Day	G	" 28,	do

Returned from Missing in Action.

Names.	Co.	Date.	Remarks.
B O Sanford	B	Oct. 10, 1864.	
J W Barnes	C		
J W Young	D		
T L Frohock	F		
T A Baker	F		

TWENTIETH REGIMENT INFANTRY.

AUGUST, 1864.

Deserted.

Names.	Co.	Date.	Remarks.
Geo W Barron	I	May 4, 1864.	
David D Bonney	I	" 4,	
Fred W McFarland	K	March 10,	

Discharged.

Peter B Merry	F	July 29, 1864.	Term expired.
Albert E Fernald	K	Aug. 1,	For promotion.

Deceased.

Isaiah Whitten	A	July 9, 1864.	From wounds received in action.
Silas Curtis	C	" 27,	do
Simon Orff	E	Aug. 28,	Of disease.
Mark A Wentworth	F		From wounds received in action.

SEPTEMBER, 1864.

Discharged.

Henry Ravel	F	Sept. 19, 1864.	Term expired.
C Welch	G	" 3,	do
George Miller	H	Aug. 31,	do
S A Winchester	K	Sept. 23,	do
Thomas Murphy	I	" 18,	do

Deceased.

Alonzo Wixon	A	Aug. 27, 1864.	Of disease.
V W Pinhorn	C	Sept. 30, 1864.	Killed in action.
W P Odlin	C	" 30,	do
S M Libby	D	" 30,	do
Lewis Carl	F	" 30,	do
Freeman Elwell	I	" 30,	do
George H Royal	K	" 30,	do
L N Monk	E	" 13,	From wounds received in action.

Transferred.

Edward B French	D	July 1, 1864.	To V. R. Corps.
Gilman L Gould	H	June 25,	do

Returned from Missing in Action.

Horace B Clark	F	Sept. 5, 1864.	At Annapolis, Md.
L Genthner	G	" 5,	do

OCTOBER, 1864.

Deserted.

Benjamin Laboree	C	Oct. 16, 1864.	To the enemy.
John D Knowles	C	" 16,	do
John B Wilson	F	" 20,	On the way to join Regt.

Discharged.

Charles R Shorey	A	Oct. 1, 1864.	For promotion.
Harrison Goding	B	July 8,	Term expired.
Andrew O'Neal	B	Aug. 31,	do
James A Philbrook	B	Sept. 6,	do
George M Wyman	B	July 9,	do

TWENTIETH REGIMENT INFANTRY, (Continued.)
Discharged.

Names.	Co.	Date.	Remarks.
Augustus Eles	B	Oct. 23, 1864.	Term expired.
George H Wood	C	" 8,	For promotion.
Arad Thompson	C	" 8,	do
David M Overlock	E	" 22,	do
Wm W Witham	F	" 7,	Term expired.
Wm A Soule	F	" 16,	do
J C Stanchfield	G	" 5,	do
R M Bailey	G	" 5,	For disability.
Horace Wyman	H	" 11,	Term expired.

Deceased.

Samuel Freeman	B	Aug. 30, 1861.	Of disease.
Wm N Jackson	B	Oct. 1,	From wounds received in action.
Joseph E Hatch	C	" 2,	do
Hugh Gates	C	" 4,	Of disease.
Randall B Morton	D	" 15,	From wounds received in action.
S A Carpenter	D	Sept. 21,	do
Oliver French	D	Oct. 1,	do
Wm H H Hasey	E	Sept. 28,	do
Charles L Place	F	Oct. 28,	Killed in action.
James A Horton	H	" 4,	From wounds received in action.
Geo B Sterling	I	" 19,	do
Geo A Ramsdell	K	" 21,	do

Transferred.

James H Miller	K	Oct. 11, 1864.	To V. R. Corps.

TWENTY-FIRST REGIMENT INFANTRY, (9 months.)

Mustered into the U. S. service at Augusta, Me., on the 13th day of October, 1862, and mustered out at Augusta by Lieut. F. E. Crossman, 17th U. S. Infantry, on the 25th day of August, 1863, on account of expiration of term of service.

TWENTY-SECOND REGIMENT INFANTRY, (9 months.)

Mustered into the U. S. service at Bangor, Me., on the 18th day of October, 1862, and mustered out at Bangor by Lieut. F. E. Crossman, 17th U. S. Infantry, on the 14th day of August, 1863, on account of expiration of term of service.

TWENTY-THIRD REGIMENT INFANTRY, (9 months.)

Mustered into the U. S. service at Portland, Me., on the 29th day of September, 1862, and mustered out at Portland by Lieut. F. E. Crossman, 17th U. S. Infantry, on the 15th day of July, 1863, on account of expiration of term of service.

TWENTY-FOURTH REGIMENT INFANTRY, (9 months.)

Mustered into the U. S. service at Augusta, Me., on the 16th day of October, 1862, and mustered out at Augusta by Lieut. F. E. Crossman, 17th U. S. Infantry, on the 25th day of August, 1863, on account of expiration of term of service.

TWENTY-FIFTH REGIMENT INFANTRY, (9 months.)

Mustered into the U. S. service at Portland, Me., on the 29th day of September, 1862, and mustered out at Portland by Capt. Francis Fessenden, 19th U. S. Infantry, on the 10th day of July, 1863, on account of expiration of term of service.

TWENTY-SIXTH REGIMENT INFANTRY, (9 months.)

Mustered into the U. S. service at Bangor, Me., on the 18th day of October, 1862, and mustered out at Bangor by Lieut. F. E. Crossman, 17th U. S. Infantry, on the 17th day of August, 1863, on account of expiration of term of service.

TWENTY-SEVENTH REGIMENT INFANTRY, (9 months.)

Mustered into the U. S. service at Portland, Me., on the 30th day of September, 1862, and mustered out at Portland by Lieut. F. E. Crossman, 17th U. S. Infantry, on the 17th day of July, 1863, on account of expiration of term of service.

TWENTY-EIGHTH REGIMENT INFANTRY, (9 months.)

Mustered into the U. S. service at Augusta, Me., on the 18th day of October, 1862, and mustered out at Augusta by Lieut. F. E. Crossman, 17th U. S. Infantry, on the 31st day of August, 1863, on account of expiration of term of service.

TWENTY-NINTH REGIMENT INFANTRY, VET. VOLS.

August, 1864.

Discharged.

Names.	Co.	Date.	Remarks.
Henry B Furbish	B	June 27, 1864.	For disability.
John Young	C	" 30,	do
Leonard G Jordan	C	Aug. 6,	do
Joseph Hume	E	July 7,	do
Leander Brooks	F	" 19,	do
James W Church	F	June 30,	do
Alonzo B Crockett	G	" 23,	do
Francis B Butters	G	July 24,	do
Wm H Bigham	H	June 29,	do
Henry Sanborn	I	" 27,	do
James E Magner	K		do
James H Walker	K		do
Alpheus L Greene	S. Maj.	July 25, 1864.	For promotion.

Deceased.

Names.	Co.	Date.	Remarks.
William Keighley	A	Aug. 25, 1864.	Of disease.
Franklin Kilborn	B	June 27,	At New Orleans, La.
Samuel R Harris	B	" 18,	do
Nathan Foster	B	" 21,	do
Henry Patch	C	July 8,	At Natchez, Miss.
John Ronco	C	June 28,	At New Orleans, La.
Osgood F Floyd	C	Aug. 9,	At Annapolis, Md.
Philip Caldwell	E	" 12,	At Washington, D. C.
Thomas Johnson	E	" 7,	At Natchez, Miss.
James Wellman	E	July 7,	do

TWENTY-NINTH REGIMENT INFANTRY, (Continued.)

Deceased.

Names.	Co.	Date.	Remarks.
Amos Young	E	July 9, 1864.	At New Orleans, La.
Franklin B Cobb	H	Aug. 3,	In New York harbor.
Isaac C York	H	" 9,	At Washington, D. C.
John O Conner	H	" 2,	At New Orleans, La.
Harrison F Whitman	I	June 12,	do
Wheeler Smith	I	" 27,	do
John W Cony	I	" 28,	do
Albion P Mower	I	July 17,	do
Jonathan E Piper	I	Aug. 4,	At Pittsburg, Pa.
Charles F York	I	" 17,	At New York.
John H Haskell	I	July 22,	At New Orleans, La.
Daniel O Warren	I	" 30,	At Washington, D. C.
Owen Getchell	I	" 14,	At Natchez, Miss.
Wm I Davis	K	June 22,	At New Orleans, La.
B E Latham	K	July 23,	In Maine.
Fred A Tiffany	K	" 20,	At St. Louis, Mo.

Transferred.

W W Judkins	A	June —, 1864.	To V. R. Corps.
Daniel Downs	B	" 4,	do
Chas E Emery	B	" —,	do
Wm H Sanborn	C	May 31,	do
Edgar N Hardy	K	June 4,	do
Samuel B Mason	I	May 31,	do

SEPTEMBER AND OCTOBER, 1864.

Returns received too late for publication.

Enlisted men of companies A and D, formerly of the 10th Regiment, and afterwards of the 1st Battalion of 10th Regiment, but transferred to the 29th Regt. at date of organization, mustered out at Augusta, Me., by Capt. C. Holmes, on account of expiration of term of service. Compiled from the muster-out rolls on file in this office.

James F Tarr	A	Oct. 18, 1864.	Term expired.
Horace C Berry	A	do	do
Edward P M Bragdon	A	do	do
John Reardon	A	do	do
John Collum jr	A	do	do
James Jennings	A	do	do
Dennis Kenney	A	do	do
Geo H Brackett	A	do	do
Henry H Shapleigh	A	do	do
Henry F Cole	A	do	do
Joseph H Chappell	A	do	do
Thaddeus Cross	A	do	do
Jeremiah Donovan	A	do	do
William S Davis	A	do	do
William Dobson	A	do	do
John Dunn	A	do	do
Stephen H Dyer	A	do	do
Benj F Duran	A	do	do
Simon Giberson	A	do	do
Geo W Hatch	A	do	do
Charles Kehoe	A	do	do
Moses Leighton	A	do	do
Geo E McIntyre	A	do	do
Moses T Moore	A	do	do

TWENTY-NINTH REGIMENT INFANTRY, (Continued.)

Enlisted men mustered out, etc.

Names.	Co.	Date.	Remarks.
Archibald McDougall	A	Oct. 18, 1864.	Term expired.
Charles F Roberts	A	do	do
Daniel M Rowe	A	do	do
Charles C Rawson	A	do	do
James Staples jr	A	do	do
William Sibley	A	do	do
James Twist	A	do	do
David Ward	A	do	do
Geo W Kendrick	A	do	do
Samuel Hanson	S. Maj.	do	do
Thomas Bugbee	Q.M.S.	do	do
William Hoppins	A	Nov. 9, 1864.	do
Joseph Gould	A	" 9,	do
Ivan Leighton	A	Oct. 4,	do
Charles Makepiece	A	" 12,	do
Amos Kelley	D	" 19,	do
Garrett Moran	D	" 19,	do
Joseph G Brown	D	" 19,	do

THIRTIETH REGIMENT INFANTRY, VET. VOLS.

JUNE, 1864.

Deserted.

Charles O Bishop	G	May 15, 1864.

Discharged.

Milton E Dunn	A	May 16, 1864.	For disability.
Sylvester Abbott	C	April 21,	do
Robert Baldwin	C	May 17,	do
Nathaniel D Chase	E	" 20,	do
Sylvester S Strout	E	June 16,	do
George Delaware	E	April 22,	do
Alden Marson	G	May 17,	do
Lewis S Libby	I	" 18,	do
Nelson Sanborn	I	April 18,	do
Wm C Marr	I	May 13,	do
Nathan Ferguson	K	April 18,	do

Deceased.

Llewellyn C Vining	A	June 23, 1864.	Of disease.
J S Brown	A	" 9,	From wounds received in action.
Albert Harvey	A	" 11,	Of disease.
Jacob Gurney	C	May 27,	do
Edwin Legrow	C	" 17,	do
John Bracey	C	June 20,	do
Hiram B Stevens	D	May 12,	do
Asa W Webber	E	" 8,	In hospital at New Orleans, La.
James F Sawyer	E	" 18,	do
B Bickford	E	" 3,	do
John Merrill	E	June 19,	do
Wm C Byron	E	" 10,	do at Morganzia, La.
John W Boston	F	May 31,	Of disease.
John McInnis	F	June 12,	do
John B Lucas	G	" 1,	do

THIRTIETH REGIMENT INFANTRY, (Continued.)

Deceased.

Names.	Co.	Date.	Remarks.
Jacob E Brown	G	June 8, 1864.	Of disease.
Benj Wentworth	G	" 9,	do
Joseph W Church	G	" 17,	do
Leroy Prentice	H	April 25,	From wounds received in action.
Amaziah Curtis	H	" 29,	do
Charles M Rowe	H	May 29,	do
D R Bartlett	H	" 30,	do
Patrick Flannery	H	June 4,	do
Charles Lyons	H	" 5,	Of disease.
Dan'l P Lambert	H	" 22,	do
Jason Wakefield	H	" 23,	do
Amos H Colby	H	" 24,	do
Charles L Walker	I	" 19,	do
John L White	K	" 6,	do
Harvey Schofield	K	" 15,	do
Armstrong Webster	K	" 17,	do
Wm McLellan	K	" 18,	do

Transferred.

Samuel Newell	E	June 15, 1864.	To V. R. Corps.
Lorenzo D French	K	" 25,	To U. S. Navy.
Noah S Ames	K	" 15,	To V. R. Corps.

JULY, 1864.

Discharged.

Benj F Beale	A	June 16, 1864.	For disability.
Frank McCullough	C	May 25,	At New Orleans, La.
Thomas Myrtle	D	June 13,	do

Deceased.

John Alden	A	April 5, 1864.	In hospital at New Orleans, La.
Allen C Ford	A	" 30,	do
Turner Wade	A	May 20,	do
Asa L Berry	A	July 2,	Of disease.
Cyrus Dunn	A	" 4,	do
Jason Cutler	A	" 9,	do
Chas H Harrington	A	" 24,	do
Rufus Greely	B	April 10,	In hospital at New Orleans, La.
Albion Field	B	" 20,	do
Columbus Hussey	B	" 16,	do
Adoniram Gurney	C	" 29,	do
Geo D Hodsdon	C	July 15,	At sea.
Algernon H Scribner	C	" 3,	do
Chas H Moody	C	" 15,	do
Thomas M Davis	C	" 1,	On board hospital boat.
George M Dolley	E	April 30,	In hospital at New Orleans, La.
Chas W Titcomb	E	June 1,	do
Dana B Graves	E	July 17,	At sea.
James Harriman	F	April 18,	In hospital at New Orleans, La.
Daniel L Howe	F	May 20,	do
Charles C Witham	F	June 15,	do
Walter Tarring	F	July 7,	At Morganzia, La.
Charles H Bryant	F	" 3,	In hospital at New Orleans, La.
Alonzo W Snell	G	April 13,	do
Almon Fogg	G	" 15,	do

10

THIRTIETH REGIMENT INFANTRY, (Continued.)
Deceased.

Names.	Co.	Date.	Remarks.
Samuel S Remick	G	June 21, 1864.	In hospital at Baton Rouge, La.
Moses C Young	H	May 24,	In hospital at New Orleans, La.
Samuel Thorn	H	July 3,	At sea.
Henry Pooler	I	" 1,	In hospital at New Orleans, La.
Joseph Pitcher	K	" 5,	In hospital at Baton Rouge, La.

AUGUST, 1864.
Deserted.

Edwin A Sprague	F	July 19, 1864.	At Bermuda Hundreds, Va.

Discharged.

Leonard Abbott	B	July 26, 1864.	At New Orleans, La.
Charles Dougherty	D	" 6,	For disability.
Henry N Fairbanks	E	June 13,	For promotion.
George A Green	E	July 1,	do
James D Hawes	F	" 22,	For disability.
Geo H Cooledgo	G	June 23,	do
Frank B Gowell	G	July 18,	do
David Mitchell	G	" 22,	do
Joseph B Condon	H	June 27,	do
John H Jones	I	July 1,	do
Geo W Sweatt	K	" 23,	do

Deceased.

Augustus M Jackson	A	July 11, 1864.	Of disease.
Charles W Jordan	A	" 11,	do
Seth D Bradford	A	April 22,	do
P A Bradford	A	Aug. 7,	do
A H S Garcelon	A	" 19,	do
Joseph E Hyde	A	" 26,	Committed suicide.
Amos O Witham	A	" 4,	Of disease.
Alanson Proctor	B	July 10,	In hospital at New Orleans, La.
John Hussey	B	" 7,	do
T C Jones	B	Aug. 11,	do at Ft. Monroe, Va.
Fred I Black	B	July 20,	do at New Orleans, La.
Geo W Hubbard	B	" 18,	do at Ft. Monroe, Va.
Geo S Herrick	B	Aug. 2,	do at Natchez, Miss.
Robert H Jackson	C	" 4,	do at Washington, D. C.
Frank Stephens	C	July 29,	do at Portsmouth, N. H.
James Larrey	C	" 6,	do at New Orleans, La.
Zebulon D Greenleaf	C	" 21,	At Otisfield, Me.
Granville Waitt	C	Aug. 29,	Of disease.
Joseph W Dean	D	July 1,	In hospital at New Orleans, La.
Charles R Curtis	D	" 8,	do
Wm K Libby	D	June 28,	do
Benjamin Jordan	D	Aug. 6,	do at Washington, D. C.
W Murphy	D	" 12,	do at New York.
Luther True	E	" 6,	do at Cairo, Ill.
Russell F Raymond	E	July 2,	do at New Orleans, La.
Wm P Pollard	E	" 2,	Of disease.
O Thompson	F	Aug. 19,	do
Amos H Kenniston	F	May 3,	From wounds received in action.
Phineas W Goodwin	G	June 30,	Of disease.
Patrick A Merrick	G	July 10,	do
Waldron Hobbs	G	" 23,	do

THIRTIETH REGIMENT INFANTRY, (Continued.)

Deceased.

Names.	Co.	Date.	Remarks.
Samuel Lishness	H	June 27, 1864.	Of disease.
James E Linscott	H	July 5,	do
James A Haley	H	" 9,	do
A T Clark	K	" 4,	In hospital at New Orleans, La.
Joseph J Maxwell	K	" 4,	do
Otis Willey	K	Aug. 6,	do at Portsmouth, Va.
John Kelliher	K	" 15,	do at Chicago, Ill.
James B Pullen	E	April 29,	In hands of enemy.
Walter N Tozier	E	" 14,	do
Eugene A Pollard	E	May —,	Went down with steamer Pocahontas.

Transferred.

Geo C Cooledge	A	June 4, 1864.	To V. R. Corps.

SEPTEMBER, 1864.

Deserted.

B Taylor	G	Aug. 13, 1864.	On the march.

Discharged.

Wm F Butler	G	June 24, 1864.	For disability
Ivory L Hill	I	" 23,	do

Deceased.

A H Standley	A	Aug. 17, 1864.	Of disease.
C L Hyde	A	" 7,	do
Orville A Lessions	A	" 11,	do
Robert H Doughty	A	Sept. 5,	do
Samuel Graves	B	July 6,	do
Daniel Murch	C	" 31,	do
Lorenzo D Stevens	C	Sept. 18,	do
James H Hanson	C	Aug. 29,	do
John Wing	C	Sept. 27,	do
James Smith	C	" 11,	do
Edwin Averill	D	" 2,	do
Caleb F Ginn	D	July 17,	do
Orrin W B Perkins	D	Sept. 8,	do
Chas A Wallingford	G	July 21,	do
Ivory Guptill	G	Aug. 14,	do
James H Radcliffe	G	Sept. 6,	do
Thomas G Morrill	G	Mar. 2,	do
Albert C Donnelly	H	Sept. 5,	do
Patrick Dougherty	H	" 16,	do
Gardner L Rich	I	Aug. 12,	do
George L Stevens	I	" 15,	From wounds received in action.
Stillman White	K	" 15,	Of disease.
Calvin Cummings	K	Sept. 1,	do

Transferred.

George W Robbins	D	June 22, 1864.	To V. R. Corps.
Rodney Emery	D	" 22,	do
Joseph A Gillespie	E	" 22,	do
Henry Peyrett	K	" 22,	do

OCTOBER, 1864.

Deserted.

Simeon Scribner	C	Oct. 1, 1864.	At Otisfield, Me., while on furlough.
Charles S Fowler	F		At St. James' hosp. N. Orleans, La.

THIRTIETH REGIMENT INFANTRY, (Continued.)

Discharged.

Names.	Co	Date.	Remarks.
Josiah A Millett	B	Aug. 4, 1864.	For promotion.
Enoch C Soule	B	" 5,	For disability.
Isaac F Bowman	E	" 18,	do
Paul Euwan	E	Sept. 29,	do
Charles F Larrabee	S. Maj.	" 1,	For promotion.
Joseph D Harville	G	Oct. 1,	do

Deceased.

Elbridge M Yeaton	A	Aug. 2, 1864.	On board steamer Wagoner.
G Jordan	B	" 4,	In hospital at New Orleans, La.
William Murray	B	Oct. 2,	do at Ft. Monroe, Va.
George Campbell	D	May —,	Of disease.
Thomas Smith	D	Oct. 11,	do at Annapolis, Md.
Thomas W Ross	E	July 16,	do
Thomas A Burnell	E	Sept. 19,	do
Nathaniel Chick	F		do at Clinton, Me.
P Fernald	G	Oct. 2,	do in Maine.
William Hasey	H	Aug. 10,	do
John A Plummer	K	" 13,	do
Geo M Benson	K	Sept. 6,	do

Transferred.

Appleton N Burnell	E	Sept. 29, 1864.	To V. R. Corps.

THIRTY-FIRST REGIMENT INFANTRY.

AUGUST, 1864.

Deserted.

G H Emerson	D	
Hiram F Page	D	
William Hayes	K	June 14, 1864.
Wm J Sawyer	K	" 14,

Discharged.

L B Smith	E	Aug. 5, 1864.	
Frank Scribner	F	" 12,	For disability.

Deceased.

John Tozier	A	Aug. 3, 1864.	Of disease.
F A Cole	A	" 14,	Killed in action.
A P Russ	A		From wounds received in action.
Chas H Whittier	A	July 10, 1864.	Of disease.
Edgar J Sewell	A	" 3,	do
Wm G Pierce	A	May 12,	From wounds received in action.
J W Borden	B	Aug. 5,	do
Chas E Berry	B	" 5,	Of disease.
William Farley	B	" 6,	do
A D Bunker	D	" 1,	From wounds received in action.
David Sawyer	D	" 9,	do
A Dudley	E	" 9,	In U. S. general hospital.
A L Crane	E	" 9,	do
Joseph J Murphy	F	" 3,	From wounds received in action.
Henry W Lancaster	F		do

THIRTY-FIRST REGIMENT INFANTRY, (Continued.)

Deceased.

Names.	Co.	Date.	Remarks.
John Duffee	F		From wounds received in action.
Daniel P Peters	G	Aug. 8, 1864.	Of disease.
Henry A Terrence	G	" 13,	do
John Hunnewell	H	July 11,	From wounds received in action.

Transferred.

Allen Gow	A	Aug. 16, 1864.	To invalid corps.
Willard F Davis	G	June 31,	do

Returned from Missing in Action.

Wm W Clark	D	Aug. 2, 1864.	
B C Nye	A	" 1,	
L G Sweat	A	" 1,	

SEPTEMBER, 1864.

Discharged.

Paul Berry	A	Sept. 28, 1864.	For disability.
John A Colson	B	" 8,	do
E A Hanson	E		do
W A Murry	H	Sept. 4, 1864.	do

Deceased.

Chas S Black	A	Sept. 16, 1864.	From wounds received in action.
J L Sanborn	B	May 14,	do
E Ward	B	Sept. 9,	do
W C Young	C	" 9,	do
O A Higgins	D	July 24,	do
C A Green	D	Sept. 6,	Of disease.
J Donham	E		do
P C Farnsworth	F	Aug. 13, 1864.	do
Thomas Cuncannon	H		From wounds received in action.
Dexter Gurney	I	Aug. 28, 1864.	Of disease.

OCTOBER, 1864.

Deserted.

John S Carleton	D	May 18, 1864.	At Spottsylvania C. H., Va.
Andrew A Googings	D	" 18,	do
S P Townsend	E	Sept. 30,	From hospital at New Orleans, La.

Discharged.

Charles R Smith	H	Sept. 15, 1864.	For disability.

Deceased.

L J Smith	A	Oct. 11, 1864	From wounds received in action.
Henry Bissell	A		Of disease at Alexandria, Va.
George Henderson	D	Sept. 30, 1864.	Killed in action.
George A Storey	C	Aug. 24,	Of disease.
Benjamin K Preston	E	Oct. 4,	do
Benjamin Pero	E	Sept. 4,	do
James F Luce	E	" 30,	Killed in action.
E A Sprague	G	" 30,	do
David Ellsworth	G	July 30,	In Mt. Pleasant hosp. Washington.
Edmund Thomas	G	Aug. 20,	Of disease.

THIRTY-FIRST REGIMENT INFANTRY, (Continued.)

Deceased.

Names.	Co.	Date.	Remarks.
A S Burnham	II	Oct. 22, 1864.	Of disease.
William Cousins	I		do at Augusta, Me.
F W Sawyer	I	Oct. 9, 1864.	do do
Cyrus Yates	I	Aug. 31,	do at David's Island, N. Y.
F O Weymouth	I	Sept. 18,	do
S Y Glidden	K	" 30,	Killed in action.
Joseph Hart	K	" 30,	do

Missing.

A W Blackman	A	Sept. 30, 1864.	In action.
Aaron McCarty	B	do	do
Joseph S Rice	D	do	In action and wounded.
A S Goodale	D	do	In action.
E C Miners	D	do	do
Alonzo C Weeks	E	do	do
J A Sprague	F	do	do
F E Cook	F	do	do
S W Bates	F	do	do
O L Larraby	F	do	do
James Ryan	G	do	do
Eli Pittman	G	do	do
Chas J Lowe	H	do	do
Geo R Jenness	II	do	do
G D Penney	I	do	do
II F Dorr	K	do	do
A B Ballard	K	do	do
L B Rogers	K	do	do

THIRTY-SECOND REGIMENT INFANTRY.

August, 1864.

Deceased.

A S Farris	B	July 24, 1864.	In hosp. at Philadelphia, Pa.
Geo F Fay	B	Aug. 1,	do Washington, D. C.
Nathaniel H Fuller	B	July 30,	do Augusta, Me.
Chas II Atwood	D	Aug. 5,	do N. Y. Harbor.
O B Richardson	E	" 23,	At Jay, Me.
O O Gould	E	" 3,	In hosp. at City Point, Va.
C G Chesley	E	July 29,	do Fairfax, Va.
Wm S Tarbox	F	Aug. 17,	do Portsmouth Grove, R. I.
Geo M Manson	II	" 26,	do Alexandria, Va.
Edward W Eldridge	K	" 22,	do City Point, Va.
Henry Bowd	II.Stew July 28,		do Philadelphia, Pa.

September, 1864.

Discharged.

Samuel Whitten	F	Sept. 26, 1864.	For disability.
O P Rice	G	Aug. 18,	By order War Dept.
Joseph McKenney	G	Sept. 5,	For disability.

THIRTY-SECOND REGIMENT INFANTRY, (Continued.)
Deceased.

Names.	Co.	Date.	Remarks.
Thomas Hubbard	A	Sept. 8, 1864.	From wounds received in action.
S D Mitchell	D	Aug. —,	Of disease.
Henry C Moody	G	July 28,	do
Wm H Smith	H	Sept. 19,	do
Charles E Phillips	H	July 27,	do
W L Alley	K	Aug. 17,	do
W Goodrich	K	Sept. 1,	do

October, 1864.
Deserted.

G L Berry	I	June 15, 1864.	At Petersburg, Va.

Discharged.

George H Lee	K	Sept. 12, 1864.	For disability.

Deceased.

Samuel Smith	C	Sept. 22, 1864.	Of disease.
Wm H Smith	H	" 19,	do
Henry B Sproul	I	Oct. 21.	do

Missing.

A J Harriman	A	Sept. 30, 1864.	Probably prisoner.
Charles F Stevens	A	do	do
Charles Potter	A	do	do
Charles Robinson	A	do	do
Alonzo Carpenter	A	do	do
Charles Bowden	A	do	do
Walter Eaton	A	do	do
A Manson	A	do	do
W S Howe	B	do	do
David Sewall	B	do	do
Henry Judkins	B	do	do
M Martin	C	do	do
Charles Webber	C	do	do
John L Ham	D	do	do
Rogers A Foss	D	do	do
H K Thompson	D	do	do
J C Norris	D	do	do
Nathaniel Chadbourne	F	do	do
G L Patterson	F	do	do
Caleb Wentworth	F	do	do
George Blodgett	F	do	do
Wm L Trafton	F	do	do
Asa B Smith	F	do	do
Henry Remick	F	do	do
John Dixon	G	do	do
S T Marriner	G	do	do
M Murphy	G	do	do
J H Herrick	G	do	do
J H McIntyre	G	do	do
J L Small	G	do	do
Charles Cushman	H	do	do
Nathaniel Brock	H	do	do
John W Sanborn	H	do	do
George Ricker	H	do	do

COMPANY B, COAST GUARD INFANTRY.

CAPT. O. J. CONANT.

Stationed at Fort Foote, Maryland.

AUGUST, 1864.
Discharged.

Names.	Co.	Date.	Remarks.
William J Maxwell		Aug. 6, 1864.	For disability.

SEPTEMBER, 1864.
Deceased.

Oliver P Perrigo		Sept. 18, 1864.	Of disease.
William Vannah		" 21,	do

OCTOBER, 1864.
Discharged.

Charles E Green	Priv.	Sept. 30, 1864.	For disability.
H H Arey	do	Oct. 18,	do
Abram G Dow	Sergt.	" 18,	do
E M Keller	Corp.	" 18,	do
Oscar R Perry	Priv.	" 18,	do
Alphonzo Brown	do	" 18,	do
Otis Walker	do	" 18,	do
Chas F Harlow	do	" 18,	do
Warren Cooper	do	" 18,	do
E J Pease	do	" 18,	do
Henry A Clark	do	" 18,	do
Wm A Rackliffe	do	" 18,	do
Benjamin Jones	do	" 18,	do
John S Butler	do	" 18,	do
Isaac B Metcalf	do	" 18,	do
John M Bachelder	do	" 18,	do
Thomas Robbins	do	" 18,	do
Herman Rankin	do	" 18,	do
C S Thompson	do	" 18,	do
Richard B Grinnell	do	" 18,	do
Fred A Elwell	do	" 18,	do
Levi Walker	do	" 18,	do
Augustus Studley	do	" 18,	do
Edgar E Witherspoon	do	" 18,	do
P Thomas	do	" 18,	do
Jason Peabody	do	" 18,	do

Deceased.

Edwin L Robbins	Priv.	Oct. 5, 1864.	Of disease.
John E Jackson	do	" 5,	do
Robert I Brewster	do	" 14,	do

www.ingramcontent.com/pod-product-compliance
Lightning Source LLC
Chambersburg PA
CBHW031456270326
41930CB00007B/1031